Movie Science

Other Books by Jim Wiese

Head to Toe Science
Over 40 Eye-Popping, Spine-Tingling, Heart-Pounding
Activities That Teach Kids about the Human Body

Roller Coaster Science
50 Wet, Wacky, Wild, Dizzy Experiments
about Things Kids Like Best

Rocket Science
50 Flying, Floating, Flipping, Spinning Gadgets
Kids Create Themselves

Detective Science
40 Crime-Solving, Case-Breaking, Crook-Catching
Activities for Kids

Spy Science
40 Secret-Sleuthing, Code-Cracking, Spy-Catching
Activities for Kids

Cosmic Science
Over 40 Gravity-Defying, Earth-Orbiting,
Space-Cruising Activities for Kids

Magic Science
50 Jaw-Dropping, Mind-Boggling,
Head-Scratching Activities for Kids

Movie Science

40 Mind-Expanding, Reality-Bending, Starstruck Activities for Kids

Jim Wiese

Illustrations by Ed Shems

John Wiley & Sons, Inc.

New York • Chichester • Weinheim • Brisbane • Singapore • Toronto

Published by John Wiley & Sons, Inc.
Published simultaneously in Canada

Design and production by Navta Associates, Inc.

The publisher and the author have made every reasonable effort to ensure that the experiments and activities in the book are safe when conducted as instructed but assume no
responsibility for any damage caused or sustained while performing the experiments or
activities in this book. Parents, guardians, and/or teachers should supervise young readers
who undertake the experiments and activities in this book.

Library of Congress Cataloging-in-Publication Data:

Wiese, Jim
    Movie science : 40 mind-expanding, reality-bending, starstruck activities / Jim Wiese.
        p. cm.—(Jim Wiese science series)
    Includes index.
    ISBN 0-471-38941-2 (pbk.)
    1. Cinematography—Juvenile literature. 2. Cinematography—Special effects—
Juvenile literature. 3. Science projects—Juvenile literature. [1. Science projects.
2. Motion pictures. 3. Science—Experiments. 4. Experiments.] I. Title: Movie science,
40 mind-expanding, reality-bending, starstruck activities. II. Title.

TR851 .W52 2001
778.5'3—dc21   00-066263

Printed in the United States of America

10 9 8 7 6 5 4 3 2 1

For Elizabeth and Matthew,
and all who share my love
of television and movies

Contents

Acknowledgments

Igrew up in what many consider the Golden Age of television and the movies. My family was one of the first in our neighborhood to get an old black and white television, and I still remember inviting friends in to watch the early shows. I also remember taking the bus from my home to the downtown theaters every Saturday afternoon to watch the latest movies. Through both of these mediums I was transported to a world of fantasy that stimulated my imagination. I remember spaceships traveling to other planets and westerns where good always triumphed over evil. In those brief moments, I felt like I was really there. Little did I know that some of what I saw would later become a reality. In less than 20 years, humans did walk on the moon. And I still believe that good will eventually win over evil.

Years later, I was given the opportunity to work on the television series *MacGyver*. While on the set, I learned more about how special effects were used to enhance the story. A special thanks goes to story editor Rick Drew, Adrianne Allen, and executive producer Steven Downing, who let me see behind the scenes of a television series and helped me start an educational project with the help of Paramount Pictures, called *Super Science with MacGyver*.

There are many people who generously gave their time and experience to make this book happen. Foremost would be Scott Steynes. Scott both offered his inside knowledge and opened doors to his network of friends in the movie and television industry. Thanks, Scott.

Again, I would like to thank the team of people at John Wiley who worked to make this book a reality. I would especially like to acknowledge the work of my editor, Kate Bradford. Her professionalism in every aspect of the publishing process always brings out the best in my writing.

Introduction

Do you have a favorite movie or television show? Was there a part in it that made you wonder, How did they do that? You may not have realized it, but there is a lot of science in the creation of movies and television shows. The art and science of special effects can make for some exciting moments in movies. But did you know that the moving picture is a special effect itself? What you are seeing is actually thousands of still images, something like pictures that a camera takes. When they're lined up and flashed past your eye at a very fast speed, the still images flow together and look like real action to your eyes and brain. This basic fact makes every movie a special effects masterpiece!

So, if you're interested in movies and television and in understanding the science that makes them, you're going to love the activities suggested in this book. They are all science projects and experiments, but with a little work, they could become the start of the next movie to win an Academy Award!

How to Use This Book

This book is divided into chapters based on general areas that work together to make a movie. In each chapter, there are science projects and experiments that can be done as part of making a movie. Each project has a list of materials. You'll be able to find most of the materials needed around the house or at your neighborhood hardware or grocery store.

New in this book are activities that can be done using technology, such as a computer or video camera. Technology is rapidly changing our lives, including the way that movies are made. More powerful computers, new software programs, and innovative cameras lead the way in making movies even more wonderful. Activities in this book will show you how to use your own computer or video camera to investigate how computers help make movie magic!

Some of the projects have a section called More Fun Stuff to Do that tells you how to try different variations on the original activity. Explanations are given at the end of each group of projects. Words in **bold** type are defined in the glossary at the back of the book.

Being a Good Scientist

- Read through the instructions once completely and collect all the equipment you'll need before you start the activity or experiment.

- Keep a notebook. Write down what you do in each experiment or project and what happens.

- Follow the instructions carefully. *Do not attempt to do by yourself any steps that require the help of an adult.*

- If your project does not work properly the first time, try again or try doing it in a slightly different way. Experiments don't always work perfectly the first time.

- Always have an open mind that asks questions and looks for answers. The basis of good science is asking good questions and finding the best answers.

Increasing Your Understanding

- Make small changes in the design of the equipment or project to see if the results stay the same. Change only one thing at a time so you can tell which change caused a particular result.

- Make up an experiment or activity to test your own ideas about how things work.

- Look at the world around you for examples of the scientific principles that you have learned.

- Don't worry if at first you don't understand how the world works. There will always be new things to discover. Remember that many of the most famous discoveries were made by accident.

Using This Book to Do a Science Fair Project

Many of the activities in this book can serve as the starting point for a science fair project. After doing the experiment as it is written in the book, what questions come to mind? Some possible projects are suggested in the section of the activities called More Fun Stuff to Do.

To begin your science fair project, first write down the problem you want to study and come up with a hypothesis. A **hypothesis** is an educated guess about the results of an experiment you are going to perform. For example, if you enjoyed doing the Fog in the Bog activity, you may want to investigate dry ice further. One possible hypothesis for an experiment with dry ice could be that more fog is produced using hot water rather than cold water.

Next you will have to devise an experiment to test your hypothesis. In the Fog in the Bog example, you might create fog using water with different temperatures, and observe the results. Be sure to keep careful records of your experiment. Next analyze the data you recorded. In the Fog in the Bog example, you could create a table showing the water temperature, the amount of fog produced, and the length of time the fog was produced. Finally, come up with a conclusion that shows how your results prove or disprove your hypothesis.

This process is called the **scientific method.** When following the scientific method, you begin with a hypothesis, test it with an experiment, analyze the results, and draw a conclusion.

A Word of Warning

Some science experiments can be dangerous. *Ask an adult to help you with experiments that call for adult help, such as those that involve matches, knives, or other dangerous materials.* Don't forget to ask your parents' permission to use household items, and put away your equipment and clean up your work area when you have finished experimenting. Good scientists are careful and avoid accidents.

The Magic of Movies

How Movies Work

You may not realize it, but there is science behind many of the techniques that are used to make movies. Did you know that cartoons and movies are actually still drawings and photographs recorded on film by cameras and projected rapidly onto a screen? It's **vision,** the way your eyes and brain work together, that makes you think you see the images on the screen move smoothly. **Physiology** is the branch of **biology** that studies the function of organisms, such as humans, and their organs, including their eyes. **Chemistry,** the science that investigates matter, is also involved in movies. When movies are made they use the chemistry involved in photography. In **photography,** pictures are made by the chemical action of light on special surfaces such as film. Chemistry is also involved in some special effects, such as making fire and fog. **Physics,** the science of matter and energy and how they interact, is also involved in making movies. Motion is part of physics, and the film must move through the camera at just the right speed to make the motion seem normal. Moving the film faster makes the actions seem faster, while moving the film slower makes the actions seem slower. Another aspect of physics is **optics,** the study of how light behaves. You need to know something about light to make good pictures.

If you want to learn more about how science is involved in making movies, try the activities in this chapter.

PROJECT 1
Pinhole Camera

With the snap of a picture, you can save a moment in time forever. Have you ever wondered how cameras work? All cameras produce images by focusing light onto film. Try making your own camera to see how! Build your own camera out of a shoe box.

Materials

shoe box   tape
aluminum foil   scissors
wax paper   pin

Procedure

1. Cut a 1-inch (3-cm) square in one end of the shoe box. Tape a piece of aluminum foil over the square. Make sure all edges of the foil are taped to the box.

2. Cut the opposite end off the shoe box.

3. Put the lid on the shoe box and tape it in place.

4. Tape a piece of wax paper over the end of the shoe box that has been removed.

5. Take a pin and make a small hole in the center of the aluminum foil.

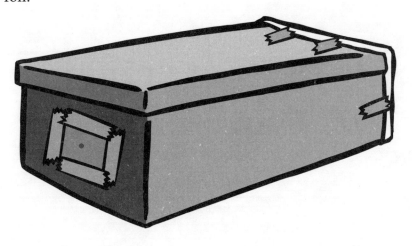

6. Point the pinhole end of the shoe box at a window or other light source. Look at the wax paper end of the shoe box. An image will pass through the pinhole and be shown on the wax paper. What do you see?

More Fun Stuff to Do

Try making the camera by using boxes of different sizes. Does the size of the box have an effect on the image that shows up on the wax paper?

Explanation

An image will appear on the wax paper. However, the image will be upside down.

Cameras, including your shoe box camera, work because light travels in a straight line. In your camera, light travels in a straight line through the pinhole and onto the wax paper. The image you see on the wax paper is upside down because light from the top of the object travels in a straight line through the pinhole to create an image on the bottom of the wax paper. Similarly, light from the bottom of the object winds up on the top of the wax paper. The image is upside down.

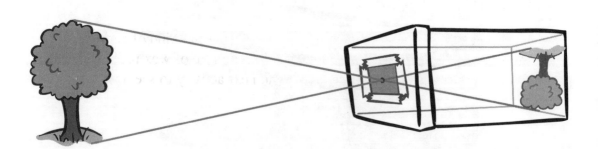

Movie Science in Action

S ince the sixteenth century, artists and scientists had been using a device called a camera obscura. Originally, it was just a room that was totally dark, with only a small opening in an outside wall. When people went into the room they saw an image of an illuminated object from outside the room. The image passed through the hole and was reproduced, upside down and in small scale, on an opposite wall, much the same as the shoe box camera you made in this activity. Artists used this image as a sketching aid. Later, a light-tight box replaced the room, and a simple lens was inserted in the hole.

In 1826, Joseph-Nicéphore Niépce used a camera obscura to project an image onto light-sensitive paper, creating in effect the first photographic camera.

PROJECT 2
Picture Perfect

In the last activity, you learned how to make a special kind of camera. But the images you made are only shown on a piece of wax paper. How can you make permanent images? Try the next activity to see how it can be done.

Materials

sheet of black construction paper
4 rocks
key

Note: This activity must be performed outside on a bright, sunny day.

Procedure

1. Place the construction paper in an open area in bright sunlight. Place a rock on each corner of the paper so that it will not blow away.

2. Place the key in the center of the paper.

3. Leave the project in the sun for at least 4 hours.

4. Remove the key and observe the paper. What do you see?

More Fun Stuff to Do

Try leaving the key on the paper for longer and shorter periods of time. How long does the paper need to be in the sun for the key to make an impression? Try the experiment on a partly sunny day. Does the key make an impression?

Explanation

The area of the paper that has been covered by the key will remain very black while the area of the paper that had the sun on it will be lighter.

Paper is made from wood fibers that have been pressed together. Construction paper gets its color from different dyes. When the construction paper is made, particles of dye dissolved in water bond or stick to the paper fibers in a chemical reaction. A **chemical reaction** is a change in matter in which substances break apart to form new substances.

A different chemical reaction occurs when sunlight hits the paper, causing the paper to fade, or lose its color. All colored paper will eventually fade if exposed to sunlight. You may have noticed this on a bulletin board at school. When pictures are removed, the areas that have been covered up have a darker color than surrounding areas.

Colored paper fades even more quickly in direct sunlight. Black construction paper in particular fades very fast because it contains the most dyes. The key, or any other object, blocks the sun and keeps the area under it from fading. After a short time, the rest of the paper fades, leaving an exact imprint of the key on the paper. You then have a picture of the key.

Movie Science in Action

In 1839, the French inventor Louis-Jacques-Mandé Daguerre (1789–1851) developed the light-sensitive daguerreotype, a photographic plate on which an image could be permanently recorded. The fundamental physical principle of photography that Daguerre discovered is that light falling briefly on the grains of certain chemicals that contain silver (silver chloride, silver bromide, or silver iodide) produces small chemical changes in the grains. When placed in certain chemical solutions known as developers, the affected grains become black.

When a photograph is taken with a camera, light reflected from the object passes through the opening in the camera and lens to form an inverted image, like the one you created in the last activity. For the brief period during which the shutter is open, the light reflecting off of this image falls on the surface of a film or plate covered by the silver chemical, causing an invisible, permanent image to be recorded on it. The developing process makes the image visible.

PROJECT 3
Thaumatrope

One of the earliest ways to make pictures move was a simple toy called the thaumatrope. This gadget makes images move so fast that you can still "see" an object that is actually out of sight. Try making one for yourself.

Materials

two 4-inch-square (10-cm) pieces of white paper
crayons or markers
two 4-inch-square (10-cm) pieces of cardboard
tape
pencil

Procedure

1. Draw a picture of a bird on one square of paper and a picture of a birdcage on the other square of paper.

2. Tape the drawings to the pieces of cardboard.

3. Tape the back of one piece of cardboard to the pencil. Then tape the other piece of cardboard back-to-back against the first drawing. The pencil will now be between the two pieces of cardboard.

4. Roll the pencil back and forth between your hands so that the thaumatrope spins. Observe the two drawings. What happens?

More Fun Stuff to Do

Think of other pairs of pictures that can come together to make one picture, such as a picture of a boat and a picture of the ocean, and make a thaumatrope out of your idea. See how many different thaumatropes you can make.

Explanation

When you spin the pencil, the two pictures that you have drawn will seem like one picture. The bird will appear to be inside the cage.

The thaumatrope creates this illusion because the hand is quicker than the eye. Your eye sees the first drawing for a fraction of a second and then it disappears. The next drawing appears before your eyes have a chance to react. The first image is retained on the retina of your eye for a fraction of a second in a process called **persistence of vision.** Images formed on the retina actually remain there for $1/30$ of a second. As a result, you see not two separate images but one image that contains both drawings. The effect of the thaumatrope is that you see both drawings together.

PROJECT 4
Flip Book

You've made two images seem like one in the last activity. What will happen if you put many images together? Try making a flip book to find out.

Materials

small pad of paper with a gummed edge
   (available at any stationery store)
pencil

Procedure

1. Before you start making your movie, you will first need to decide what it will be about. Start out with a simple idea. For example, you could make one of a boy shooting a basketball, a seed growing into a flower, or an ant walking across the page. Your movie should have a beginning, a middle, and an end, and it should be simple enough to draw easily.

2. Make at least 25 drawings to bring your movie to life. Start with the last page on your pad. This will be the first drawing because it is easier to flip your pad from back to front. Make your first drawing.

3. Turn to the next-to-last page. You will probably be able to see the previous drawing through the page, which will help you with your next one. Make your next drawing. It should be slightly different from the first one.

4. Continue drawing pictures on each page until your movie is done. Each drawing should be slightly different from the one before, and the drawings should show a simple idea from beginning to end.

5. To view the movie, hold the pad on the top edge and flip through it quickly from the last page to the first.

More Fun Stuff to Do

Try flipping the pages of your book slower or faster. What happens to the motion? Use a computer drawing program (such as Kidpix) to draw your pictures. How can the use of a computer make it easier to draw pictures where only one object is in a slightly different location to show motion?

Explanation

When you flip the pages of the book, the images appear to move in a way similar to a movie.

The flip book is another example of persistence of vision. Again, the images that are formed on the retina remain there for about $1/30$ of a second. As a result, you see not two images but one image that contains two successive drawings. The effect of the flip book is that the illustrated objects seem to move.

When you flip the book at different speeds, as suggested in More Fun Stuff to Do, you change the speed at which the images move. When you flip the book more slowly, the images seem to move more slowly. When you flip the book faster, the images seem to move faster.

The very first moving pictures were not intended to entertain an audience. Instead, Eadweard Muybridge, a British photographer, was trying to settle a bet about the way horses run. Muybridge bet that when horses run, there are times when all their feet are off the ground at the same time.

In 1877, Muybridge arranged 24 cameras near the finish line of a horse race in California. Each camera took a slightly different picture as the horses ran by. The pictures were then set side by side to settle the bet. One photograph clearly showed a horse with all four of its feet off the ground. But Muybridge noticed something else. When he quickly looked from picture to picture, it appeared to be not 24 separate pictures but a brief image of a galloping horse, due again to persistence of vision.

This simple experiment led to the development of an industry that sells over a billion movie tickets in the United States every year.

PROJECT 5
Zoetrope

In the previous activities, you have investigated how persistence of vision is used to make individual pictures seem to move. But how did the first moviemakers use this principle to make the original movies? Try this activity to find out.

Materials

thin cardboard circle with
   5-inch (13-cm) diameter

thin 4-by-16 inches
   (10-by-41 cm) cardboard strip

tape

scissors

thumbtack

pencil with eraser

colored pencils or markers

paper

Procedure

1. Position one long edge of the cardboard strip along the edge of the cardboard circle. Overlap the strip on itself if necessary and tape in place. This will create a cardboard cylinder.

2. Use the scissors to cut eight equally spaced slits along the top edge of the cylinder. Each slit should be $\frac{1}{8}$ by $1\frac{1}{2}$ inches (.5 by 3.75 cm).

3. Push the thumbtack through the center of the cardboard circle from the inside of the cylinder, then push it into the pencil's eraser. The cylinder should spin easily on the top of the pencil.

4. Cut a strip of paper that is 2 by 16 inches (5 by 41 cm). Place the strip inside the bottom of the cylinder. Cut the strip so that it fits exactly once around the cylinder.

5. Remove the strip and divide it lengthwise into eight equal areas.

6. Use the colored pencils or markers to create an animated sequence using the eight areas, similar to what you did with the flip book in the previous activity.

7. Place the strip back in the bottom of the cylinder so that the middle of each picture is aligned below one of the slits.

8. Look at the pictures through the moving slits as you spin the cylinder. What do you notice?

More Fun Stuff to Do

Try making other animated stories for use in your zoetrope.

Explanation

When you spin the cylinder and look through the holes, the pictures seem to be moving. The slits let you look at only one picture at a time.

One of the first "moving picture" machines, created in the mid-1800s, was called the zoetrope, from the Greek words *zoe,* which means life, and *trope,* which means to turn. When viewed through a series of slits in the side of a revolving cylinder, the individual pictures along its inside edge were seen as a moving picture. Once again, this was due to persistence of vision in the viewer, which kept previous pictures on the eye's retina for a fraction of a second.

Movie Science in Action

One problem with the zoetrope is that only one person can view the "movie" at a time. Thomas Edison, however, didn't find this a problem. He thought that movies were best viewed this way. So when motion pictures were later transferred to film using a process devised by George Eastman, Edison invented the kinetoscope, a film viewer that used a peephole, so that one person at a time could see it. He believed that this would make more money than showing a film to a large audience all at once.

Edison made a mistake by not extending the patents on his kinetoscope to England and Europe. Louis and Auguste Lumière designed a portable version, called the *cinématographe,* based on Edison's machine. In 1895, the movie era was officially begun when the Lumières presented a series of short films to a paying audience in the basement of a Paris café!

PROJECT 6
Moving Pictures

You have your movie and you've shown it to a few friends, but you want to find a way to show it to lots of people at the same time. What can you do? The answer is to project it on a screen or something else. Try this activity to learn an interesting way this can be done.

Materials

slide projector
one 35-mm slide
white construction paper
1 yard (1 m) length of wooden dowel

Procedure

1. Place the slide in the projector. Turn the projector on.

2. Place the construction paper about 6 feet (2 m) from the projector. Adjust the focus so that the image from the slide is clear on the white paper. Remove the paper.

3. Hold the dowel where the paper was originally located.

4. Wave the dowel rapidly up and down by flicking your wrist. What do you notice?

More Fun Stuff to Do

Try moving the dowel in different ways, such as in a cylinder or cone shape. What difference does this make?

Explanation

When you move the dowel rapidly up and down, the image will appear in the air.

Light cannot be seen unless it reflects off an object. In this case, the light strikes the moving dowel and is reflected. When this reflected light enters your eye, it makes an image on your retina. Your eye retains each piece of the image for about $\frac{1}{30}$ of a second—long enough to let you put the pieces together to make a complete picture. This action of the eye is another example of persistence of vision.

Movie Science in Action

Movies can be shown on many different materials. Movie screens work well because their white color reflects most of the light that strikes them. However, movies can be shown on other materials as well. In a recent live Disney on Parade extravaganza, part of an animated Mickey Mouse cartoon was shown on a spray of water!

PROJECT 3-D

Humans see with two eyes positioned close together on the front of the head. The fact that we have two eyes positioned in this way is very important to the way we see the world. But how does this fact affect the way that movies and television are made? Try this activity to find out.

Materials

colored pencils or markers
plain white paper
cardboard box
tape

thin cardboard
scissors
glue
Plasticine or modeling clay

Procedure

1. Use the colored pencils or markers and a sheet of paper to draw a background for an outdoor scene. It could include mountains, trees, and even a river.

2. Tape the scene to the back of the cardboard box.

3. On another sheet of paper, draw and color a human figure. Glue the figure to a piece of thin cardboard, then use the scissors to cut it out.

4. Use Plasticine or modeling clay to create a base for the figure so that it stands by itself.

5. Place the figure about 1 foot (30 cm) in front of your background scene.

6. Stand with your head about 2 feet (60 cm) from the background scene. Close your left eye. Look at the figure and scene, using only your right eye.

7. Next, close your right eye and look at the figure and scene, using only your left eye.

8. Alternate eyes quickly while looking at the figure and background scene. What do you notice about the figure's position in front of the scene?

9. Next place the figure flat on the background scene and repeat steps 6 to 8. What do you notice about the figure's position in front of the scene this time?

Explanation

When the figure is set away from the scene, it will appear to move left and right as you view it with either eye. However, when the figure is flat against the background, it will not seem to move.

Because humans have two eyes facing forward, we see things in three dimension (3-D). Most of what your right eye sees is also seen with the left eye. Each eye sees the object from a different angle and has a slightly different view of an object that is in front of you. These images are created in each retina and sent to the brain. The brain superimposes these two images, one on top of the other. The combination of these two different views into one picture gives a 3-D image. But when the figure is right next to the background, this does not occur because both eyes see exactly the same picture and the figure has a flat appearance.

Because movies and television shows are shown on flat screens, we do not see 3-D images created by our different views from each eye. There are other ways that movies create depth and the 3-D effect.

Movie Science in Action

Some movies and television shows have sought to create a 3-D experience using a flat screen. To do this, scenes are recorded with special cameras that record two slightly different pictures of a scene, similar to the way your eyes see. When the pictures are seen with the naked eye, you see two distinct images. But when the pictures are viewed through glasses with special lenses, you see the picture in 3-D. The lenses allow each eye to see only one of the images. The brain superimposes the different pictures and again creates depth in what you see.

PROJECT 8
Keep It in Perspective

There are many situations where the background helps to set the scene for a movie. Representing the three-dimensional aspects of a background has always been a challenge to a set designer. Perspective drawings are one way to give a three-dimensional look to a drawing. But how can you make a set seem bigger than it actually is? Try this activity to learn how it is done.

Materials

ruler
paper
pencil

Procedure

1. Use the ruler to draw a horizontal line on a sheet of paper. Place two points, A and B, near the ends of the line. These two points represent the vanishing points of the drawing.

2. Draw a vertical line, about ¼ the length of the horizontal line, through the middle of the horizontal line. Label the top of the line C and the bottom D.

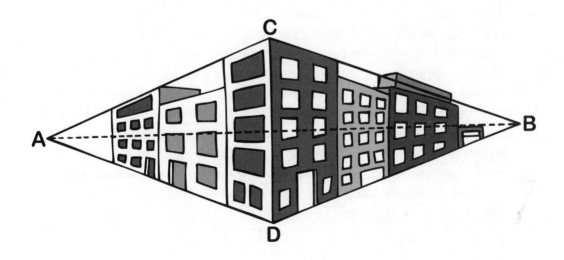

3. Connect A and B to C and D. These will serve as guides for your perspective drawing. For variation in the heights of the tops of buildings, lines can be added that are parallel to these lines.

4. You are going to create a street scene that gives the illusion of three dimensions. Add vertical lines and begin to draw buildings and details using the perspective lines as an aid. How does a perspective drawing give the three-dimensional aspect to the structure?

More Fun Stuff to Do

Use paints to color the street scene you just drew. Maybe paint in some figures on the sidewalk. How do you make people near the horizon look farther away? How realistic can you make your scene?

Explanation

Your drawing should appear to have a three-dimensional quality. The buildings will seem to extend off to the horizon.

This activity uses two-point perspective to create the three-dimensional quality of the scene. Over time, your brain learns to judge perspective based on an expectation of the relative sizes of certain objects. An object that appears large must be close. If the same object appears small, it must be farther away. If you look down a tree-lined street, the trees look smaller and the road looks narrower the farther down the street you look. If you draw a picture that uses this same perspective, parts of the picture will appear to be farther away than others, simply because of their changing size. Although every point of the picture is actually the same distance from the eye, the brain interprets some parts of the picture as farther away and other parts as closer to the viewer.

A ctors are sometimes shorter than they appear to be in movies. To make small actors seem taller, sets are made smaller. In one of Universal Studio's sets, one side of a western street was made to a smaller perspective, while the other was made larger. When the hero stepped out of the sheriff's doorway on the smaller side of the street, his head almost touched the top of the doorway, making him appear larger than life. But when the bad guys came out of the saloon's doorway on the larger side of the street, their heads were much lower compared to the top of the doorway, making them appear much smaller.

PROJECT 9
Distorted Room

The evil Dr. Distructo's assistant towers in the doorway and seems at least 7 feet tall! Is the actor really that tall, or can movies use other means to make a shorter person seem tall? Try this activity to find out.

Materials

plain white paper
ruler
felt pens
cardboard
books

2 small plastic figures—about 2 inches (5 cm) tall (one slightly smaller than the other)
Plasticine or modeling clay

Procedure

1. Place a sheet of paper horizontally in front of you. Use a felt pen and a ruler to draw a vertical line 4 inches (10 cm) long near the edge of the paper. Place a mark at each inch (2.5 cm) along the line.

2. Draw another line 6 inches (15 cm) long perpendicular to the first line that begins in the middle of the first line and extends across the paper. Place a mark at each 1.5 inches (3.75 cm) along the line.

3. Draw a third line parallel to the first line. This line should be 2 inches (5 cm) long, with its center on the line in step 2. Place a mark at each one-half inch (1.25 cm) along the line.

4. Connect the top of the line from step 1 with the top of the line from step 3. Similarly, connect the bottom of the line from step 1 with the bottom of the line from step 3.

5. Draw a line connecting the marks between the end lines.

6. Draw vertical lines parallel to the line in step 1 that go through each of the marks you made on the 6-inch (15-cm) line so that your finished drawing is similar to that below.

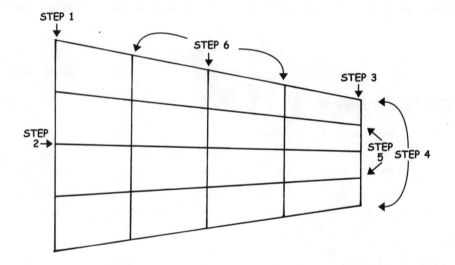

7. Fold the paper along the bottom line of the figure so that it makes a right angle.

8. Place the paper on a piece of cardboard so that the figure you drew is standing up perpendicular to it. Place a book behind the paper so that it stands up. Cover the edge of the first piece of paper with another piece of paper to make a floor for the room.

9. Stack several books on the table, then place one end of the cardboard on the books so it creates an incline. Add enough books to make the vertical lines on the paper vertical to the room.

10. Stand the taller plastic figure near the shorter vertical line and the smaller figure near the longer vertical line. Use Plasticine or modeling clay if necessary to hold the figures in a vertical line.

11. Place your eye near the higher corner of the cardboard and look at the figures. Which one looks larger?

12. Reverse the figures so that the taller figure is near the longer vertical line and the smaller figure is near the shorter vertical line.

13. Again place your eye near the corner of the cardboard and look at the figures. Which one looks larger this time?

Explanation

The taller figure placed near the shorter line will look even taller than the smaller figure. When you place the smaller figure near the shorter line, then it seems taller than the taller figure.

This is an example of forced perspective. **Forced perspective** is a kind of optical illusion. Illusions such as this one occur because your brain incorrectly interprets something you are seeing to be something similar to what you've seen before. Your brain assumes that the horizontal lines are parallel and therefore that the distance between them is the same, so the figure that covers more lines is taller.

Movie Science in Action

The movie *Jaws* is about a gigantic white shark that attacks a town and its inhabitants. The movie was made using a large mechanical shark as well as actual shark footage. But the movie producers could not find a real shark as big as their mechanical monster, and the mechanical shark couldn't move around as well as a real shark. So when they wanted to film the shark attacking a man in a cage under water, they hired a four-foot-nine-inch ex-jockey to stand inside a scaled-down shark cage during part of the filming. This made the real sharks seem much bigger than they actually were.

Making It Real

Props and Makeup

When you look at a good movie or television show, you seem to be transported to a different place and time. If the props, costumes, and makeup are effective, then the story seems more real. Science can help make this part of the movie or television show more lifelike.

Moviemakers use chemistry to make fake blood, and they have to know something about biology to accurately portray wounds or body parts. A fire you see in the movies can be simulated and controlled using chemistry. And physics will tell you that your hero is going to have to pretend that the fake boulder he just picked up is really heavy.

Try the activities in this chapter to investigate some of the ways that science is used to make movies look real scary!

PROJECT 1
Rock On

Unexpectedly, the X-ray machine turns on and the hero is given a dose of radiation that knocks him out. When he awakes, he has superhuman strength. He can pick up large boulders with ease. But how can the actor do it? Try this activity to find one way.

● Materials

sample rock the size of your fist

6-inch (15-cm) cube of Styrofoam (available at most craft stores)

penknife

paints the colors of your sample rock

paintbrush

adult helper

Procedure

1. Look at the sample rock. What shape is it? What color is it? Use this rock as a model for this project.

2. With adult supervision, use the knife to carve the Styrofoam cube into the rock's shape by first cutting the corners off and giving it a rounded shape, then continuing to cut as necessary.

3. Use the paint to color the Styrofoam so that it looks like your rock. You will probably need to use several colors and painting techniques to get the right look.

4. Set your "rock" next to the sample rock. Lift each. Now pretend the Styrofoam rock is real. How would you lift it differently?

5. Show a friend the two rocks. Can he or she spot the fake?

Explanation

Your "rock" should look similar to a real rock but should be much lighter.

The weight of an object depends on its size and density. **Density** is the ratio of the mass of an object to its volume. If two objects are the same size (volume), the object with less mass is less dense than the object with more mass. By using materials that are less dense but shaped and colored to look like the original material, movies and television shows can make you think their heroes have superhuman strength.

Styrofoam or other light building materials are often used in movies to create props of objects that would be too heavy in real life. For example, if you see a ceiling fall on a person or a brick wall collapsing, they are made not of stone but of some lightweight material such as Styrofoam. They look real, but their low density makes them very light, so the actors squished under them do not really get hurt!

PROJECT 2
Strange Reactions

The secret agents look at the mysterious white powder they have found. If it is what they think it is. . . . They test it to be sure, placing a few grains of the white powder in a clear liquid. The liquid immediately turns red. They look at each other and worry how they are going to stop the fiendish plan. We know the white powder really isn't anything dangerous, but how do the moviemakers get it to change colors so it seems that way? Try this activity to find out.

Materials

red cabbage
2 quarts (2 liters) of tap water
1 2-quart pot
strainer
plastic bowl
5 small jars
marking pen

1 teaspoon (5 ml) lemon juice
1 teaspoon (5 ml) vinegar
1 teaspoon (5 ml) bottled water
1 teaspoon (5 ml) baking soda
1 teaspoon (5 ml) ammonia
adult helper

Procedure

1. Tear two red cabbage leaves into small pieces. Ask your adult helper to boil them for five minutes in the 2 quarts (2 liters) of water.

2. Put the strainer over a plastic bowl and have your helper pour the mixture through the strainer. Throw the leaves away. Allow the colored liquid to cool in the plastic bowl.

3. Set up five small jars and pour a half cup (125 ml) of the cooled cabbage juice into each. Number the jars 1 through 5 with the marking pen.

4. Add the lemon juice to jar 1, the vinegar to jar 2, the bottled water to jar 3, the baking soda to jar 4, and the ammonia to jar 5. **Caution: Be careful not to spill the ammonia on your hands. If you do, wash immediately with soap and water.**

5. Observe the color that each chemical turns the cabbage juice and record the color on a chart similar to the one below.

Jar No.	Substance	Acid/Base	Color
1	lemon juice	acid	
2	vinegar	slightly acid	
3	bottled water	neutral	
4	baking soda	slightly base	
5	ammonia	base	

6. Use the remaining cabbage juice to test foods in your kitchen, such as milk, pickle juice, soy sauce, baking powder, etc. Set up new jars of cabbage juice and add pieces of food. Observe the color the juice becomes.

Based on the color, use your chart to determine whether the food is acid, slightly acid, neutral, slightly base, or base.

More Fun Stuff to Do

Try mixing other solutions with the cabbage juice. Try using liquids other than cabbage juice to test the substances. For example, try tea, grape juice, etc.

Explanation

Here are the expected results for your experiment:

Jar No.	Substance	Acid/Base	Color
1	lemon juice	acid	red
2	vinegar	slightly acid	pink
3	bottled water	neutral	dark purple
4	baking soda	slightly base	light green
5	ammonia	base	green

A **chemical indicator** is a special substance that, when mixed with an acid or a base, will change color. Being an acid or a base is a chemical property of a substance. An **acid** is a substance that reacts with a base to form a salt, while a **base** is a substance that reacts with an acid to form a salt. Cabbage juice is a chemical indicator, so it will change color depending on the type of solution that is added.

Movies will use a liquid changing colors to indicate all sorts of things, from the results of a drug test to just adding props in a scientist's laboratory.

PROJECT 3
Hidden Jewels

A giant diamond has been stolen from one of the guests at a weekend party. The police let no one in or out and make a thorough search of the house, but they do not find the missing gem. The guests are all brought into the room where the diamond was last seen. The famous detective reveals where the diamond has been hidden since it was first taken—visible yet invisible. How is it possible? Try this activity to find out.

Materials

2 glass jars
water
Wesson oil (regular, not lite)
glass eyedropper

dish towel
Pyrex stirring rod (available
   from most science stores)

Procedure

1. Fill one jar half full with water.

2. Fill the other jar half full with Wesson oil.

3. Look at the glass eyedropper out of the water. Immerse it in the water, squeeze the bulb, and fill it with water. How does the glass portion of the dropper look in the air and how does it look in the water?

4. Take the glass eyedropper out of the water, dry it, and put it in the Wesson oil. Squeeze the bulb and fill it with the oil. Now how does the way the glass portion of the dropper look compare to how it looked in the air?

5. Put the Pyrex stirring rod in the water. What does the part of the rod sticking out of the water look like compared to the part in the water?

6. Take the Pyrex stirring rod out of the water, dry it off, and put it in the Wesson oil. How does the rod look above the oil and how does it look in the oil?

More Fun Stuff to Do

Try different clear liquids, such as corn syrup, mineral oil, or other brands of vegetable oil, to see if they can make either the eyedropper or Pyrex rod disappear.

Explanation

You will be able to see the glass eyedropper in both water and oil, although its image will be slightly blurred in the liquids compared to the air. You will be able to see the Pyrex rod in water, but not in the oil.

Transparent objects, such as glass, Pyrex, water, and oil, let light pass through them. However, when light strikes a transparent object, such as glass, the light **refracts,** or bends, as it moves from air to the glass and from the glass back into the air. The amount that light refracts, or bends, depends on the **index of refraction** of the transparent object. Water and glass have different indexes of refraction. When the difference between the indexes of refraction of two transparent materials is great, transparent objects will be more visible. But when the differences between the indexes of refraction of the two transparent materials is small, no refraction takes place between the object and the liquid, and the object in the liquid will seem invisible. Because the indexes of refraction for Wesson oil and Pyrex are similar, you will not be able to see the Pyrex stirring rod below the surface of the liquid.

In the scene described at the beginning of this activity, the diamonds were sitting in a glass filled with a clear liquid that had the same index of refraction as the diamonds, so no one could see them.

PROJECT 4
Animal Attraction

During a scene in a movie children are playing in a playground when suddenly a swarm of bees attacks them. How did the director know when the bees were going to come around, and how did he get them to leave after they were no longer needed? Try this activity to learn how movie crews can control insects.

Materials

blindfold (such as a handkerchief)   small paper cup
something that has a nice scent   paper towel
   (e.g., perfume or vanilla extract)   helper
cotton balls   large room

Note: Ask your parents for permission before moving any furniture when you do this activity.

Procedure

1. Have your helper give you a hand pushing the furniture against the walls of a large room.

2. Soak several cotton balls in the scented substance. Place the cotton balls in the paper cup.

3. Blindfold your helper. Have her smell the cup with the cotton balls.

4. Put the cup with the cotton balls on the opposite side of the room.

5. Have your helper try to find the cup by using her sense of smell.

More Fun Stuff to Do

Repeat the activity using different smell cups, each containing a different scented substance. Which smell was easiest to find? Which smell was the most difficult?

Explanation

Your helper should be able to find the cup after a little time. While our sense of smell is not as good as some animals', it is still remarkable.

One current theory about how we detect smells is that the shape of the molecule we smell helps us identify the smell. An odor molecule that is sniffed into the nose will only fit into a specific shaped site in the nose, similar to the way a key fits into a lock. Once the odor molecule is fitted into the site in the nose, a message is sent to the brain, and we sense a specific smell. Each receptor site in the nose is shaped specifically for a different smell. The human nose can detect between 2,000 and 4,000 different odors produced by various combinations of the smell receptors in the nose. As good as our sense of smell seems, other animals have a much more developed sense of smell than ours.

Wranglers are the people who train animals to perform in movies and television. They use other methods besides smell to get animals to act the way they want them to. Dogs and cats will lick sweet substances off the faces of actors, while rats will "attack" a person covered with peanut butter.

An episode of the TV show *X-Files* included a scene where a teacher and her children are attacked by a swarm of bees while playing in a playground. To get this scene to work without harming anyone, a pheromone was applied to the teacher and certain areas of the playground. A **pheromone** is a chemical that an animal can smell and is attracted to. Bees were attracted to the pheromone, and it also made them less inclined to sting. The bee wrangler released a swarm of bees. They were immediately attracted to the pheromones, swarming to the teacher and playground, creating the effects of an attack. When the scene was over, the wrangler called the bees back to their nest using the same pheromone while all pieces of the equipment, and the teacher, were washed with soap and water.

PROJECT 5
Blood Simple

Many movies use blood to make a movie very scary. Of course, all of the blood you see in movies is fake! There are many different recipes for fake blood. Try this activity to find out one way blood can be made.

Materials

measuring spoons
white corn syrup
cup
water

toothpick
red food coloring
cornstarch
soy sauce

Procedure

1. Place 2 tablespoons of white corn syrup into a cup.

2. Add 1 tablespoon of water to the cup. Stir with the toothpick.

3. Add 2 drops of red food coloring to the cup. Again stir the mixture with the toothpick.

4. Add a pinch of cornstarch and several drops of soy sauce to the mixture. Again stir the mixture with the toothpick until all substances are completely blended.

5. Place a small amount of this mixture on the back of your hand. What does it look like?

Explanation

The mixture that you made looks a lot like blood. This fake blood is similar to the one that is used in television and movies.

Although this recipe is simple, real blood is a very complicated substance. Blood is 55 percent plasma. **Plasma** is the liquid part of blood that is mainly salt water. In addition to the plasma, blood is made up of three different kinds of blood cells. About 44 percent of blood is red blood cells. **Red blood cells** carry oxygen to all of the cells in the body and carry carbon dioxide away. Less than 1 percent of blood is white blood cells. **White blood cells** help the body fight infection and disease. Less than .01 percent of blood is the **platelets,** which helps blood clot to heal cuts and tears.

The movie *Psycho* was originally filmed in black and white. In the famous shower scene, you see "blood" running down the bathtub drain. Since Alfred Hitchcock, the director, didn't need the blood to be red, he used chocolate syrup. Now the next time you see blood in the movie *Psycho,* maybe it will be less scary if you just keep saying, "It's only chocolate syrup. It's only chocolate syrup."

PROJECT 6
Scabs

If blood isn't gross enough, maybe you want to cover your actor with scabs. The makeup department will be happy to put fake ones on in the right places. Try the next activity to learn one way that this can be done.

Materials

measuring spoons
petroleum jelly
plate
fake blood from Blood
   Simple, project 5

toothpick
tissue paper
cocoa powder
paper towel

Procedure

1. Place a tablespoon (15 ml) of petroleum jelly on the center of the plate.

2. Add a teaspoon (5 ml) of the fake blood to the jelly and stir with the toothpick.

3. Transfer enough of the mixture to the back of one of your hands to make a spot about the size of a quarter.

4. Tear a circle slightly smaller than the size of a quarter from the tissue paper and use it to cover the mixture on the back of your hand.

5. Place another small layer of the mixture on top of the tissue paper.

6. Sprinkle some cocoa powder over the mixture. What does it look like?

7. To remove your fake scab, wipe the back of your hand with a paper towel.

More Fun Stuff to Do

Try mixing 1 1/2 cups of oatmeal and 1/4 cup of water into a thick paste. Let a small amount of mixture dry on your hand. What does the dry mixture look like? Try adding other things to the mixture, like food coloring. Can you make your mixture look more real or scary?

Explanation

Your fake scab holds fake blood together in a way similar to the way a real scab forms. The oatmeal mixture, from More Fun Stuff to Do, looks like dead, rotting, or diseased skin.

The platelets in your blood help the blood clot to heal cuts and tears. Trillions of fragile platelets move through the blood vessels.

If platelets strike a rough surface, such as part of a blood vessel torn in a cut, the platelets break apart and release a chemical that forms thin protein threads. These threads, like the tissue paper in your fake scab, wrap around the damaged area, trapping blood cells and sealing the cut in the skin. This framework prevents red blood cells from passing through it. However, white blood cells can travel through it so they can kill off any infection that might get through your skin.

Movie Science in Action

The type of oatmeal mixture you used in the More Fun Stuff to Do section is used in other movie special effects as well. When Linda Blair "vomited" in the movie *The Exorcist*, the gross substance she spat out was made out of split pea soup and oatmeal!

PROJECT
He Got Me!

The knife is slowly dragged across the hero's skin, and blood trails behind it as the cut develops. You know he's not really being cut, so how did the moviemakers make the "blood" appear in just the right place? Try this activity to see how this special effect is done.

Materials

dull butter knife
fake blood from
   Blood Simple, project 5

eyedropper
tape

Procedure

1. Fill the eyedropper with the fake blood.

2. Hold the eyedropper against the flat part of the butter knife so that the tip of the eyedropper is near the tip of the knife.

3. Tape the eyedropper in place. Make sure that the tape is only on one side of the knife.

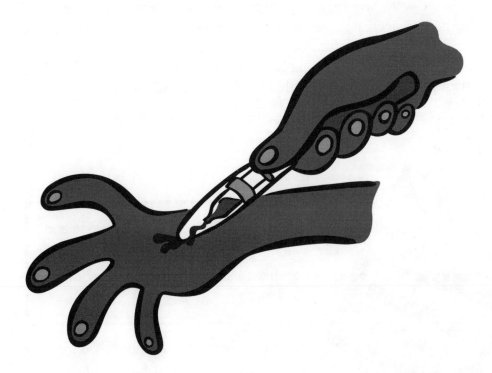

4. Hold the knife against the skin on the back of your hand so that you can touch the bulb of the eyedropper at the same time. Hold the knife so that you cannot see the eyedropper on the other side of the knife.

5. Slowly and lightly move the knife across your skin. As you do, squeeze the bulb of the eyedropper. What happens?

Explanation

When you move the knife across your skin and squeeze the bulb of the eyedropper, the fake blood gets pushed out in a line, and it appears that the knife is cutting you.

What you have created in this activity is a prop the movie industry calls a "blood knife." It is used to create the illusion that a knife is cutting someone, when it actually is only leaving a line of blood from a concealed bulb.

Fluids move from the bulb because of Pascal's principle. **Pascal's principle,** discovered by the seventeenth-century scientist Blaise Pascal, says that if pressure is exerted on one part of a fluid, then the pressure is transmitted everywhere in the fluid. When you squeeze the bulb, it decreases the volume of the bulb and thus increases the pressure on the liquid inside of it. This pressure is transmitted everywhere in the fluid, including the fluid in the eyedropper tube. When the pressure reaches the fluid in the tube, it pushes the fluid out of the tube and onto the skin.

Movie Science in Action

In addition to the blood knife, television and movies also use a "squib vest" to make it appear that an actor is bleeding after being injured. The squib vest is used when someone is supposed to have been shot. The actor or actress who is going to be shot wears a squib vest under his or her clothes. At one or more places on the vest there is a small packet of blood. Behind the packet of blood is a small explosive charge that can be triggered electronically. When a gun filled with blanks is fired at the actor or actress, a special effects technician explodes the charge, releasing the blood through the clothes, so that it looks as if a bullet from the gun struck the person.

3 Did It Really Happen?

Special Effects

Special effects designers use many different kinds of science to create scenes that aren't real. They use their knowledge of sound, weather, computers, machines, and much more to make what you experience on the screen seem just like real life, or even larger than life!

To learn more about movie special effects, try the activities in this chapter.

PROJECT 1
Sound Effects

Films, television, radio shows, and live plays use sound effects to make their stories realistic. The person who adds these sounds to the show is called a **foley artist.** Some sounds are recordings of the real objects being used. But some sounds are produced in other ways. Try the next activity to learn how this can be done.

Materials

wax paper
small bowl
salt
dried peas
large plastic bowl

thin, flexible cookie sheet
hair dryer
empty soda bottle
helper

Procedure

1. Gather all the materials together and practice the sounds, using the suggestions given below.

   • Rain—Make a large cone out of wax paper and hold it at an angle. Put a bowl under the bottom of the cone to catch the salt. Sprinkle salt from the top of the cone so that it runs down the inside.

- Ocean waves—Put ¼ cup (65 ml) of dried peas into the large plastic bowl. Tilt the bowl slowly back and forth so that the peas slide along the bottom from side to side.

- Thunder—Hold the metal cookie sheet by one end and shake it.

- Jet plane—Run the hair dryer at low speed.

- Foghorn—Blow across the top of the soda bottle.

2. Have your helper read the story below while you add the sound effects.

Story: One Day at the Beach

"It looked like a great day to go to the beach. The sky was sunny and there wasn't a cloud around. In the distance, I could hear a jet plane [jet plane sound effect] take off from the airport. The waves on the beach [ocean waves sound effect] were fun to play in. I was playing with my friends, and we didn't notice that the weather was beginning to change until it was too late. Soon the clouds began to roll in and the rain started [rain sound effects]. Thunder crashed all around us [thunder sound effects]. We all ran for cover. As we huddled under our beach towels all we heard was a foghorn in the distance [foghorn sound effects]. We knew that our day at the beach was over."

More Fun Stuff to Do

1. Try other ways to make sounds effects, and invent your own special effects.
2. Write your own story and make it more realistic by using these or other special effects.
3. Record and use other sound effects. For example, you can use a tape recorder to record the sound of a car driving past you.
4. You can also download sounds from the Internet or use sounds that are included with your computer's operating system.

Explanation

In this activity, you were the foley artist, who adds sound effects to a story in order to make it more realistic. Our ears are great at distinguishing among sounds, but sometimes our brains are fooled by sounds that are similar.

Sound is energy that we can hear. Sound happens when an object vibrates and causes the air molecules around it to vibrate. These sound **vibrations** travel through the air, causing anything they hit to vibrate as well.

When sound vibrations reach your ears, sensitive structures within the ear react to the vibrations, causing you to hear the sound. The ear can be divided into three sections: the **outer ear,** the **middle ear,** and the **inner ear.** The outer ear is composed of the outer ear flap, the **pinna** (what you commonly call the ear), which collects the sound, and the **ear canal,** or **auditory canal,** which connects and directs the sound vibrations to the delicate parts of the ear located inside your head.

The middle ear begins at the **eardrum.** The eardrum moves when sound vibrations hit it. The vibration of the eardrum causes the three

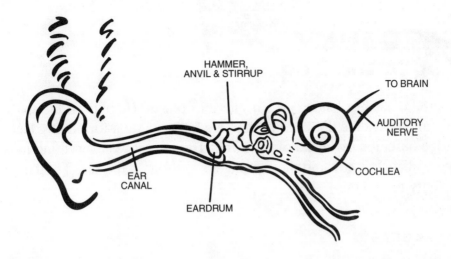

HAMMER,
ANVIL & STIRRUP

TO BRAIN

AUDITORY
NERVE

COCHLEA

EAR
CANAL

EARDRUM

bones of the middle ear to move as well. These bones are called the **hammer,** the **anvil,** and the **stirrup,** so named because of their shapes. Because of the bones' shapes and their orientation, the vibration is **amplified,** or made louder, as it moves to the inner ear.

The sounds vibrations finally reach the **cochlea** in the inner ear. The cochlea is a fluid-filled chamber that contains specialized hair cells that respond to sound waves of different vibrations. Information from these cells travels through the **auditory nerve** to the brain, where the sound is identified.

Movie Science in Action

Although many television comedy shows are filmed in front of a live audience, others use effects similar to foley art to enhance the show. Technicians will add a "laugh track" of taped audience laughter at certain times in the show to try to reinforce the parts of the show that are supposed to be funny.

PROJECT 2
Fog in the Bog

Our hero has just landed on a mysterious planet. He puts on his space suit and opens the door of the ship. He looks out at a forbidding landscape obscured by layers of thick fog. The fog makes everything look more alien, but how did the filmmakers get fog on the set? Try the next activity to find out.

Materials

baking dish
warm water
small plastic animals
winter gloves

dry ice (look under "ice" in the Yellow Pages)
adult helper

Warning: Do not touch the dry ice with your bare hands!

Procedure

1. Place the baking dish on the table.

2. Fill the dish with warm water until it is about ½ inch (1.25 cm) deep.

3. Place the plastic animals so that they are standing in the water.

4. Have the adult helper put on the winter gloves and then place several small pieces of dry ice in the water. Wait for several minutes and watch. What happens?

More Fun Stuff to Do

Create a mad scientist's potion! Put a few drops of food coloring into a glass of water. Have your adult helper add dry ice to the glass of water, and see what happens.
Caution: Do not drink the water.

Explanation

The scene will become filled with a fog that was created by the dry ice.

What we call "dry ice" is actually frozen carbon dioxide, the same gas that we exhale when we breathe out. Carbon dioxide freezes at −60°F (−50°C). (Which is why it is important not to touch it with bare hands. It is so cold that it could freeze your skin if you touched it for longer than a few seconds.)

When the dry ice is put into warm water, it changes from a solid to a gas in a process called sublimation. **Sublimation** is when a solid turns directly into a gas without turning into a liquid first. As the carbon dioxide gas is formed, it bubbles through the warm water. The carbon dioxide bubbles cause some of the warm water to turn into a cold water vapor, which rises to the surface of the water as fog. This is similar to what happens when you exhale a warm breath on a cold day.

PROJECT 3
A Frosty Morning in July

You are making a television show about Christmas, but you have to film in July! How do you make it seem like it's cold outside? You already have some fake snow to blow around, but to complete the scene you want to have frost on the windows. Try this activity to find out one way to do it.

Materials

Epsom salts
   (available at drugstores)
dark construction paper
hot water
cup

teaspoon
paintbrush
flat piece of glass (This can be
    borrowed from a picture frame,
    but be sure to ask first!)

Procedure

1. Pour a few grains of Epsom salts onto the construction paper and look at them closely. What do they look like?

2. Add a half cup (125 ml) of hot water to the cup.

3. Add one teaspoon (5 ml) of Epsom salts to the water and stir until dissolved. Keep adding one teaspoon of Epsom salts at a time until no more will dissolve and a layer of salts begins to collect at the bottom of the cup.

4. Dip the paintbrush into the top half of the Epsom salt solution and paint a layer of solution around the edges of the piece of glass.

5. Wait for the solution to dry. What does the glass look like? How do the crystals on the glass compare to the shape of the grains that you first took out of the box?

Explanation

As the solution dries on the window, the water evaporates and the Epsom salt crystals remain stuck to the glass. It will look as if frost has collected on the glass.

Crystals are the regular shape that some solids have. Crystals can have cube, diamond, or even more complex shapes. Epsom salts have a diamond shape. When water vapor in the air condenses and freezes on a cold window, it creates frost, or ice crystals. The advantage of using chemicals other than water to make the crystals on the window is that Epsom salts will not melt in July!

PROJECT 4
The Nailboard

"Catch that woman!" a voice yells. The detectives race down the hall, never once letting their quarry out of their sight. They're almost up to her when she disappears behind the closing elevator doors. The detectives look up and helplessly watch as the lights click off the floors and the criminal gets away. But is the elevator really going down? Try the next activity to find out.

Materials

an old string of small Christmas tree lights (Ask an adult if you can use them. You'll have to cut them up for this activity!)
wire cutters
5 small flathead nails
hammer
2-by-4-by-6-inch (5-by-10-by-15-cm) piece of wood
two size D batteries
electrical tape
adult helper

Procedure

1. Hammer the nails in a line partway into one side of the board. There should be about 1 inch (2.5 cm) between each nail.

2. Be sure the string of Christmas lights is *not plugged in!* Use the wire cutters to cut the wire halfway between six of the lights on the end farthest from the plug end. You should end up with five lights with two wires extending from each.

3. Ask your adult helper to use the wire cutters to remove a half inch (1.25 cm) of the plastic insulation covering from the end of each piece of wire.

4. Use the wire cutters to cut a 10-inch (25-cm) piece of wire from the plug end of the Christmas tree light string. Ask your adult helper to remove the insulation from the ends of this piece, as they did in step 3.

5. Tightly wrap the end of one wire from each light around a different nail on the board.

6. Take the other wires from each light and wrap the ends all together. Tape this group of wires securely to the top end of one of the batteries. Tape the second battery to the first battery, so that the top of the second battery is touching the bottom of the first.

7. Tape one end of the long wire to the bottom of the second battery.

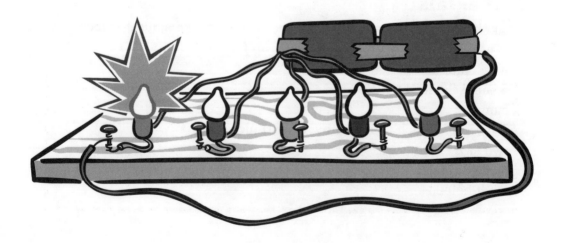

8. Touch the other end of the long wire to the top of one of the nails. What happens?

9. Touch the long wire to the top of each of the nails, one after the other in the line. What happens?

Explanation

When you touch the long wire to the top of the nail, a light will light up. When you move the wire from nail to nail, the light connected to the nail you are touching will light up.

In this activity you created a device called a nailboard. Sometimes a movie will create a part of a set that looks like an elevator. The actress gets into the elevator, the doors close, but the elevator doesn't go anywhere. Instead, using a device similar to the nailboard, the lights go on in sequence to make you think the elevator is moving down floors.

Movie Science in Action

In addition to turning on lights in sequence, a nailboard can also be used to ignite explosive charges. You may have seen a movie in which an airplane fires a burst of bullets at someone who is running on the ground. The bullets appear to hit in a line just along side of the hero, barely missing him.

To get this effect, special effects designers bury under the ground a series of small explosive charges wired in a line. An electric signal is then used to set off the charges. As the hero runs by the buried charges, a special effects technician touches a wire to the nail heads and sets off the charges. The charges kick up a bunch of dust in just the right spots to look as if the bullets have hit there.

PROJECT 5
Lightning Strikes

As the rain begins to fall harder and harder, the children run in from outside, laughing and dripping. Through the window, you see a jagged flash of lightning. Moments later a loud clap of thunder sounds, and everyone screams. The filmmakers didn't just wait for a thunderstorm, so how did they make it look like there was lightning outside? Try the next activity to see one way lightning can be created.

Materials

paper towel   balloon
crisped rice cereal   wool sweater

Procedure

1. Place the paper towel on the table.

2. Put the cereal on the paper towel.

3. Blow up the balloon and knot the end.

4. Rub the balloon several times on the wool sweater.

5. Bring the balloon near the cereal. Observe what happens.

More Fun Stuff to Do

With shoes on, rub your feet along the carpet in the house. Move toward a door. Reach for the doorknob with your index finger. What happens? Try this activity on days with different weather conditions, such as rainy, hot and dry, cold and dry, etc. Does it work better in one kind of weather than another? Try it in the dark to see the spark jump from your fingers to the doorknob.

Explanation

The cereal will jump up and stick to the balloon. In More Fun Stuff to Do, an electric spark will jump from your hand to the doorknob, giving you a small shock.

Both the original activity and More Fun Stuff to Do use **static electricity,** which is electricity that does not flow. Static electricity builds up with friction, which occurs when two objects, such as wool and a balloon, rub together. All objects are made of atoms, and every atom has an equal number of protons and electrons. **Protons** have a positive charge, and **electrons** have a negative charge. When these charges are equal, an object is neutral or uncharged. Some objects, however, such as wool or hair, easily lose electrons. When you rubbed the balloon with the wool, some electrons moved from the wool to the balloon. The balloon then has a negative static charge.

When you bring the negatively charged balloon near the cereal, the negatively charged balloon repels (pushes away) the electrons in each piece of cereal. The electrons move to the opposite side of the cereal. This gives the side of the cereal nearest the balloon a positive static charge. The positively charged end of the piece of cereal is attracted to the negatively charged balloon. The cereal is so light that the attractive force is enough to pull it up to the balloon.

One of nature's most spectacular forms of static electricity is lightning. Lightning is simply an enormous spark caused by huge amounts of static electricity. Electrons collect on certain kinds of clouds, called thunderclouds, as they move through the air, giving them a negative charge. When the electric charge on these clouds is large enough, an electric spark travels from the cloud to the positively charged Earth.

As the lightning spark travels through the air, it heats the air, causing it to expand rapidly. When this expanded air returns after the spark has passed through it, the sound it makes is the thunder we hear.

Fake lightning is created in many different ways on movie sets. Simply turning lights off and on can create the effect of lightning Other ways include creating lightning using spark generators capable of creating large static sparks, adding computerized lightning to the scene, or mixing the shot with actual lightning on film.

PROJECT 6
Twister!

The sky gets blacker and blacker. Our heroes jump in their trucks and speed right into the heart of the storm. Suddenly, on the horizon is a giant tornado twisting into their path. Real tornadoes are rare and very dangerous. So how do filmmakers create them for the movies? Try the next activity to learn how.

Materials

2 half-gallon (2-liter) plastic soda containers (empty and clean)
tap water

1-inch (2.5-cm) metal washer
duct tape

Procedure

1. Fill one of the containers two-thirds full of water.

2. Place the metal washer over the opening in the container.

3. Turn the second container upside down, and place it on the washer.

4. Use the duct tape to securely fasten the two containers and the metal washer together. Use several layers of tape to make sure that there will be no water leaks when you turn the bottles over.

5. Turn the bottles over so that the bottle with the water is on top.

6. Make a wind sound. Hold the bottles tightly and shake them quickly in a small circle. Then stop, and watch what happens.

Explanation

The water will spin in a circle as you spin the bottles. As the water from the top bottle moves into the bottom bottle, it will form a "twister" shape. Even when you stop spinning the bottles, the water will continue to twist.

There are two forces at work in this activity. (A **force** is a push or a pull.) One force is **gravity,** the force of attraction between all objects. Gravity pulls all objects to Earth, including water. Gravity pulls the water in the top bottle toward the bottom bottle. The air in the bottom bottle also exerts a force. When you first turned the bottles over, some of the water in the top bottle flows into the bottom bottle but then stops. The force of the air or air pressure in the bottom bottle stops the flow of the water.

When you swirl the bottles, a small tornado forms. In the center of the water tornado is a hole. The hole goes from the top of the water to the opening between the two bottles. The hole allows air from the bottom bottle to escape to the top bottle. As the air escapes from the bottom bottle, the air pressure in the two bottles becomes equal. Gravity is then the only force acting on the water, so the water flows down into the bottom bottle.

When the water is in the top bottle, it has potential energy. **Potential energy** is energy that is stored for later use. When you swirl the bottles, you give the water movement, or kinetic energy. **Kinetic energy** is energy that is being used. As the water swirls from the top bottle to the bottom bottle, it changes its potential energy into kinetic energy. The movement of the water from the top bottle to the bottom bottle helps to keep the water spinning in the tornado effect.

Movie Science in Action

When they made the movie *Twister*, they had to create tornadoes. Instead of using water, they created them with water vapor and fans. As the water vapor rose, fans above it caused it to spin, creating the tornado effect.

PROJECT
Computer Images

The use of computers has made moviemaking easier. Computers can add features like a futuristic building or a hideous monster to a movie. They can alter images and even remove parts of a scene. Try this activity to see how computers can help moviemakers.

Materials

computer   Internet connection (optional)
computer paint program

Note: The exact operating instructions for each computer paint pro-gram may differ and may not be exactly as demonstrated here.

Procedure

1. Copy an image file of a person from the Internet or your hard drive.

2. Open and paste the computer paint program image onto a blank page.

3. Alter the image of the picture using various computer paint tools. For example, change the size of the picture by dragging the corner size boxes, use the erase tool to erase the background of the picture leaving only the person, change the color of the person's eyes using a colored pencil, or give the person glasses or a mustache using the drawing tool.

4. Draw your own background scene for the picture, then color your background scene using the paint can tool.

5. Try other ways to alter the picture. Flip the picture horizontally, then vertically.

6. Try using other computer programs, such as a Kai Goo program, to alter the image by distorting or stretching it one way or the other.

Explanation

You should be able to easily alter the picture in many different ways.

Computers have made making movies easier. When the original *Star Wars* movie was made, George Lucas revolutionized the movie industry by using computers to add such visual effects as light saber rays and missile shots from fighting spacecraft. His company Industrial Light and Magic still does computer special effects for many movies.

We think of science fiction and animated movies as having lots of computerized special effects, but the movie *Braveheart,* set in medieval England, had the most computer effects of any movie in 1996. The computer was used not to add effects but to take things away. Computers were used to remove from the film anything that gave the appearance of modern times. Computers erased jet trails in the sky, electricity and telephone wires in the distance, and even a shopping mall that sat near a battle scene!

PROJECT 8
Robot Hand

In the movie *Ghostbusters,* two huge, scary-looking "terror dogs" come to life on the top of an apartment building. How can moviemakers make these dogs and other lifelike models move in ways that make them seem real? Try this activity to see how it can be done.

Materials

scissors
ruler
$8\frac{1}{2}$-by-11-inch ($21\frac{1}{2}$-by-28-cm) piece of cardboard
nail
2 wire brads

wire coat hanger
pliers
2 paper clips
walnut-size ball of modeling clay
adult helper

Procedure

1. Place your hand flat on the table so your palm is down. Carefully watch your hand as you flex your index finger and move it toward your hand.

2. Cut three pieces of cardboard, each 11 by 2 inches (28 by 5 cm).

3. Use the nail to make a small hole in each end of each piece of cardboard. Center the holes about 1 inch (2.5 cm) from the end.

4. Line up the cardboard pieces as shown in the diagram, with the first hole of the second piece covering the second hole of the first piece and the first hole of the third piece covering the second hole of the second piece.

5. Insert the brad in each of the overlapping holes through both pieces of cardboard. Bend back the ends of the brads to attach the cardboard pieces, but do not attach them so tightly that the pieces are unable to move.

6. Have an adult unbend and straighten the coat hanger and then use the pliers to make a small loop at one end of the wire.

7. Insert the wire loop through the second hole in the third piece of cardboard as shown.

8. Test the movement of the cardboard finger by holding on to the opposite end of the finger and moving the coat hanger wire. Adjust the attachments until the finger moves freely.

9. Use the coat hanger wire to move the finger. Try to make the finger move the way your finger moved in step 1. Can you do it? What problems do you have?

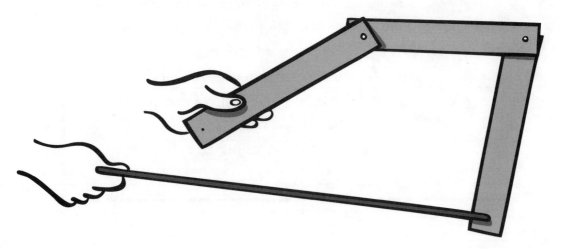

More Fun Stuff to Do

Try making another machine that could imitate another part of a body.

Explanation

The cardboard finger will have actions similar to the flexing of a real finger.

The cardboard finger you made is a **simple machine** (a device that helps you to do work more easily) called a lever. A **lever** is made up of a rigid board or bar that is supported at a fixed point called a **fulcrum.** Actually, the cardboard finger is a series of levers. The cardboard pieces are the rigid boards, and the wire brads are the fulcrums. Levers make it easier to lift heavy loads because they magnify the force exerted; in other words, they turn a small force into a big one. When you pull just a little bit on the wire, you create a big movement of the mechanical finger. Levers can also magnify distance.

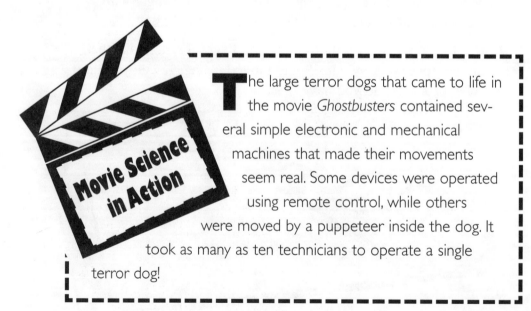

Movie Science in Action

The large terror dogs that came to life in the movie *Ghostbusters* contained several simple electronic and mechanical machines that made their movements seem real. Some devices were operated using remote control, while others were moved by a puppeteer inside the dog. It took as many as ten technicians to operate a single terror dog!

PROJECT 9
The Strongest Human Alive

The giant gorilla stands very still. When he slowly opens his hand we see a full-grown woman standing on his palm. No gorilla is really that big, so how did they make it look like the woman is standing on his hand? Try this activity to see one way it can be done.

Materials

set of stairs outdoors
2 helpers

Procedure

1. Have the first helper walk up the stairs so he stands at the level of the second helper's waist.

2. Have the second helper walk about 2 yards (2 m) away from the first helper.

3. Walk about 5 yards (5 m) away from the second helper, then face both helpers.

4. Have the first helper stand with his feet together.

5. Have the second helper lift one arm up along the side of her body with her palm up.

6. Ask the helpers to move until the palm of the second helper is directly below the feet of the first helper. What does this effect look like?

More Fun Stuff to Do

Try having the two helpers add action without spoiling the effect. For example, the second helper could look as if she is straining to hold a very heavy weight, or the first helper could stand from a squatting position. How do these actions help with the effect?

Explanation

It should look as if the first helper is standing in the palm of the second helper.

This effect is caused by the way eyes judge distances. Although each eye gives a slightly different view of the scene, the difference between the two views grows less and less as the distance from the object increases. As the distance from an object increases, the brain begins to use the difference in the size of the objects to help decide what is closer and what is more in the background.

This effect is also created because what we see in front of us is actually a composite, or combination, of several pictures that travel from the eye to the brain. You move your eyes three to five times per second, scanning different areas in front of you, creating different pictures of what is there. You remember the objects you've just seen, and the brain combines the different images into one picture.

In this effect, your brain puts the separate parts of the picture together and assumes that both figures are the same distance away. Your brain then interprets the scene to be a very strong woman holding a man in the palm of her hand.

PROJECT 10
Slo Mo

Superman flies across the sky in the blink of an eye—faster than a speeding bullet! Cut to Lois Lane falling slowly out of a high window. How do moviemakers make things seem to move faster or slower than normal? Try this activity to find out.

Materials

thread spools   hammer
scrap wood   rubber bands
nails   adult helper

Procedure

1. Hammer two nails partway into the piece of scrap wood. Place equal-size thread spools on each nail, as shown below. Stretch a rubber band around the spools.

2. Turn one spool. What happens? If you turn the spool one full turn, how much does the other spool turn? In what direction does it turn relative to the first spool?

3. Take the rubber band off of one of the spools, twist it once, and put it back on the spool. Turn one spool. What happens this time? If you turn the spool one full turn, how much does the other spool turn? In what direction does it turn relative to the first spool?

4. Replace one of the spools with a larger spool and repeat steps 1 and 2. Try turning first the small spool, then the large spool. What happens?

5. Hammer a third nail into the board and place a spool on it. Experiment with three spools and rubber bands. What do you discover?

Explanation

When you turn one of the same-size spools, as in step 1, the second spool turns the same amount and in the same direction. When you twist the rubber band, the spools still turn the same amount, but the second spool turns in the opposite direction from the first. When you use a larger spool and turn the smaller spool, the larger spool will turn less than the smaller spool. If you turn the larger spool, the smaller spool turns more than the larger spool.

In this activity, you have created a belt-and-wheel system. A belt-and-wheel system can be used to transfer circular, or rotational, motion from one shaft to another. In doing this, the system can change the direction of the applied force, the magnitude of the force, or the speed of the force.

When two similar-size wheels are connected directly by a belt, the turning of one wheel will cause the other one to also turn. If the two wheels are the same size, they will turn the same amount for each turn. This means they turn at the same speed. If the belt between the two is twisted, the second wheel goes in the opposite direction.

However, if the wheels are different sizes, the amount they turn will be different. Over a set period of time, the smaller wheel will make more turns than the larger wheel. The smaller wheel would turn faster, and the larger wheel would turn slower. In this way, wheels and belts can be used to change the speed of motion.

Systems of wheels and axles, belts, gears, and pulleys move film through cameras and projectors. Different-size wheels move the film quickly or slowly through the camera and the projector. This is how filmmakers make Superman move at twice the normal speed. A film editor combines a speeded-up film of Superman flying with background scenes filmed at regular speed.

Helping the Camera

Light and Color

In addition to knowing about the science subjects you already investigated in the previous chapters, a person making a movie also needs to know about optics. **Optics** is the study of light and how it behaves. This includes colors as well as how light reflects and refracts.

When we normally think about light, we think of white light. But white light is actually composed of many different colors of light. English scientist Sir Isaac Newton was one of the first to investigate light. Newton passed a thin beam of light into a **prism** (a transparent object that bends light). He was astonished to discover that when the light left the prism it was no longer white but had spread into its component colors—red, orange, yellow, green, blue, indigo, and violet. This was the first step to discovering how and why we see in color.

To learn more about how an awareness of the properties of light and color helps moviemakers, try the activities in this chapter.

PROJECT 1
Sunset

The heroine's face has a golden glow as she watches the cowboy ride off into the sunset. A fragment of the sun's orange light reflects off the single tear running down her face. Did the filmmakers wait for the perfect lighting, or is there another way to reproduce the look of a sunset? Try this activity to find out.

Materials
large glass jar

water

flashlight

milk

teaspoon

Procedure

1. Fill the jar three-fourths full of water.

2. Shine the flashlight into the water from the left side of the jar. Look at the beam from both the side facing you and the side opposite the light (the right side). What do you notice about the color of the light in each case?

3. Place 1 teaspoon (5 ml) of milk in the water and mix with the teaspoon.

4. Shine the flashlight into the mixture from the left side of the jar. Again look at the beam from both the side facing you and the side opposite the light (the right side). What do you notice about the color of the light in each case this time?

Explanation

When you look at the light shining through the plain water, the light will appear white from both sides. But when you add milk to the water, the light will appear blue from the side facing you and yellow-orange from the side opposite the light.

This activity shows what happens to sunlight when it travels through the atmosphere, the air surrounding Earth. Sunlight is white light made up of all the colors of the **spectrum**—red, orange, yellow, green, blue, indigo, and violet. When sunlight travels through the atmosphere, it hits molecules of gas and dust particles, similar to the milk particles in the jar. The blue light of the spectrum is affected most by these particles, so it is scattered or reflected in both the sky and the milk solution. When this scattered blue light hits your eyes, the sky during the day looks blue. This is the same reason that the milk solution looks slightly blue when looked at from the side of the jar facing you. When we look at the sun setting on the horizon, or after it passes through the milky solution, the light is traveling through a large part of the atmosphere, and most of its blue color has scattered, leaving mainly the red and yellow colors. In the same way, the white light that has to pass through the milk particles has its blue light scattered off to the side, so you see red-orange light through the end opposite the light.

To reproduce the lighting of a sunset, filmmakers place red and yellow filters, called gels, over the lights on the set.

PROJECT 2
What's Really There?

The townspeople chase the vampire up into the mountains. They catch up to him and trap him next to a sheer rock face. Suddenly, as their flickering torches light up his face, he laughs, pulls his cape up over his eyes, and disappears! Try this activity to simulate a method movies used to make things seem to disappear.

Materials

chair

handheld mirror, about 4 by 6
   inches (10 by 15 cm)

white wall

helper

Procedure

1. Have your helper sit in the chair next to the white wall so that
his left side is about 1 foot (30 cm) from the wall. Ask him to sit
perfectly still.

2. Stand about 3 feet (1 m) in front of your helper.

3. Hold the bottom of the mirror with your left hand and put the
mirror edge against your nose, so that the reflecting surface of
the mirror faces sideways, making a 45-degree angle toward the
white wall.

4. Keeping the mirror edge against your nose, rotate the mirror until your right eye sees just the reflection of the white wall while your left eye sees the face of your helper.

5. Move your right hand in front of the white wall, as if wiping the surface with a cloth. Continue to look at the wall and your helper at the same time. What happens to your helper's face?

More Fun Stuff to Do

Try reversing this activity so that your left eye looks in the mirror and your right eye looks at your helper. Is there any difference in what happens?

Explanation

When you first get the mirror adjusted, you will see both your helper and your moving hand. However, after a short time, the face of your friend will begin to disappear, and you will see only your moving hand.

Normally, your two eyes see only very slightly different pictures of what is in front of you. However, holding the mirror the way you did causes you to see two very different pictures. Your left eye sees your helper, while your right eye sees the reflection of your hand moving in front of a white wall. Your brain tries to put these two pictures together so that they make sense as one image. At first, your brain combines bits and pieces of both pictures. However, your brain is very sensitive to motion. Since what your left eye sees (your helper) does not move, your brain emphasizes the motion that the right eye sees, so parts of your helper's face will begin to disappear. No one knows exactly why parts of the face sometimes remain.

It is important to note that this activity does not work in the same way for everyone. Since one eye is dominant over the other, a reverse setup, as suggested in More Fun Stuff to Do, may work better. But for some people, this activity will never work.

Movie Science in Action

When movies want to get this same effect, the director will film two scenes, similar to the two different pictures you looked at in this activity. The two scenes are then superimposed (one put on top of the other) using a computer. By slowly switching from one scene to another, an object can be made to appear or disappear. For example, in the vampire scene mentioned earlier, the filmmakers would take a picture of the same scene both with and without the actor playing the vampire. They would then superimpose the two films and gradually switch from the scene with the vampire to the scene without the vampire. The vampire has disappeared!

PROJECT 3
Ghost Images

As the young boy enters the deserted house, he remembers the rumors about the ghosts that live there. Feeling afraid, he tiptoes down the entry hall and turns on the overhead light. There is a soft, scraping sound to his right, and he turns to see his own reflection in the window. But suddenly next to him in the reflection he sees another image. It's a ghost! Or is it? Try this activity to find out.

Materials

window on the first floor
    of a house
overhead light

flashlight
helper

Note: This activity should be done at night.

Procedure

1. Have your helper stand outside the house, about 5 feet (1.6 m) from the window, facing the house and looking inside.

2. Turn the overhead light off inside the house. Have your helper turn the flashlight on and shine it onto his face. Stand about 6 feet (2 m) from the window and look out. What do you see?

3. Next, turn the overhead light on inside the house and have the helper turn off the flashlight. Again look out the window. What do you see now?

4. Finally, turn the overhead light on inside the house. Look out the window. Have your helper turn the flashlight on. What happens?

Explanation

When the lights are off inside the house and there is a lighted object outside, you can see the object. However, when the lights are on inside the house and there are no lights outside, the window acts like a mirror and you see only your reflection and nothing from outside. If the light is turned on outside while the light is on inside, then you will see both images, superimposed on each another.

Light can do several things when it strikes an object. Two things it can do are reflect (bounce off the object) or transmit (pass through the object). When the lights are off inside the house the light reflected off your helper's face will be transmitted through the glass, and you will see your helper outside. When the light is on inside the house and there is no light outside, the light inside the house will reflect off the surface of the glass, and you will see an image of what is inside the house and nothing outside. But when the lights are on inside the house and also outside the house, the reflected image and the transmitted image combine, creating an effect that can look like a ghost.

PROJECT 4
More Ghostly Images!

"Mirror, mirror on the wall. Who's the fairest of them all?" the evil queen asks. But when she looks in the mirror, her own image is replaced with that of Snow White. How can this happen in a movie? Try this activity to see one of the many ways this can be done.

Materials

1-by-1-foot (30-by-30-cm) square piece of window glass

1-by-1-foot (30-by-30-cm) piece of aluminized Mylar reflecting film
   (available at most hardware stores)

duct tape

2 2-by-4-by-12-inch (5-by-10-by-30-cm) pieces of wood

long rubber bands

2 gooseneck desk lamps

2 dimmer switches (ready-to-use type that lamp plugs into)

adult helper

Procedure

1. Have your adult helper place the reflecting film on one side of the glass following the instructions given with the film.

2. Have your adult helper cover the edges of the glass with duct tape to avoid cuts from any sharp edges.

3. Place the pieces of wood on opposite sides of the bottom of the glass and hold them in place with the rubber bands. This will form a mirror stand.

4. Stand the mirror in the middle of a table.

5. Place the gooseneck lamps on the table, near the glass and facing away from it in opposite directions.

6. Connect each lamp to a dimmer switch and plug the switches into a wall outlet.

7. Sit across the table from your adult helper with the glass in between. Both of you should be the same distance away from the glass.

8. Dim the lights in the room. You should be able to see both your helper's face and your own face in the mirror.

9. Line up your faces so that your nose and eyes are in about the same place on the glass.

10. Turn on both lamps so that they are very dim. Make sure that each is pointed toward one of your faces.

11. Change the dimmer switch so that you have more light while keeping your helper's dim, then reverse, so that your light is dim while your helper's is brighter. What happens?

Explanation

When you turn the lights brighter on your side of the glass, your helper's face will disappear and only your face will be visible. When your light is dimmed and your helper's light is brightened, your face will slowly disappear and your helper's face will become visible.

When you add the Mylar film to the glass, you create a two-way mirror. The mirror reflects about half of the light that hits it and transmits, or lets pass through, the rest of the light. If your light is bright, then the amount of light that reflects from your face is greater than the amount of light that is transmitted from the dimly lit helper's side. But when your light is dim and your helper's light is bright, then the light from the helper's side that is transmitted is greater than the small amount of light from your side that is reflected.

Movie Science in Action

When detective shows use two-way mirrors for viewing a line-up or an interrogation room, the room the police stand in is dim while the room the criminals stand in is brightly lit. This lets the police or a witness view the criminal without their being seen by the bad guy!

PROJECT 5
Addition by Subtraction

Look, up in the sky! It's a bird! It's a plane! It's a special effect! From *Superman* to *The Rocketeer,* movies have been able to make it appear that people can fly. But how can they do it? Try this activity to learn one way.

Materials

see-through folder covers in
   clear, blue, and red plastic
magazines (optional)
colored markers

paper
scissors
glue

Procedure

1. Find pictures of clouds or the tops of buildings from a magazine or use the colored markers to draw a background scene on white paper. (The background should be of a place where a person might fly.)

2. Cut out the scenery and glue it to the front of the clear plastic folder.

3. On another piece of white paper use the colored markers to draw a person who appears to be flying. Color the person in. Use scissors to cut out the picture of the person.

4. Place the blue plastic over the clear plastic with the background. Glue the flying person on the blue plastic so that he appears to be flying over the background.

5. Reverse the order of the plastic sheets so that the blue sheet is on the bottom and the clear background sheet is on the top.

6. Hold the red plastic sheet in front of your eyes and look at your picture. What happens?

7. Continuing to look through the red plastic, slide the blue plastic sheet slowly from side to side. Does it make it seem like your person is flying over your background?

More Fun Stuff to Do

You may have varying success, depending on the quality of the plastic used in the activity. If it doesn't work well the first time, repeat the effect by gluing the person to green plastic and using yellow plastic to look through. Will these colors work differently? Try different combinations of colored plastic until you get the best results.

Explanation

When you look through the red plastic at the person on the blue plastic, the person will look about the same, but the blue background will turn very dark. Sliding the blue plastic sheet will make it appear that the person is flying over the city. This activity simulates the science behind a movie technique known as blue screen. Blue screen allows filmmakers to combine two scenes into one.

White light is a mixture of all the colors of the spectrum: red, orange, yellow, green, blue, indigo, and violet. When light strikes an object, some of the light is reflected and some of the light is absorbed. An object that reflects red light and absorbs the other colors is seen as red. An object that reflects blue light and absorbs the other colors is seen as blue.

But clear objects also transmit light. The color of a transparent object depends on the color of light it transmits. A red piece of plastic appears red because it absorbs all the colors that make up white light, except red, which it transmits. A blue piece of plastic transmits blue light.

Thus, the red plastic acts like a filter. A red filter will absorb blue light and let other colors pass through. The light that is reflected off the blue plastic could not get through the red filter, and so the background looks very dark.

These color properties also help explain why a new color is created when two different paint colors are mixed. For example, blue paint reflects not only blue light but also green and violet. Yellow paint reflects red, orange, yellow, and green. When blue paint and yellow paint are mixed, the only common color that is reflected is green. (Blue paint + yellow paint = green paint.) The other colors have been subtracted (actually absorbed) by the paint.

Movie Science in Action

Movies often use this property of light. They will first film the actors in front of a blue screen. This part of the movie can then be "added" to a background scene and the blue color easily "subtracted" through the use of a filter. In the movie *Star Wars: The Phantom Menace*, several of the fight scenes were first filmed in front of a blue screen. Then the fight scene was added to a painted background scene to make it appear that the fight was in a different location.

PROJECT 6
Night and Day

The two children move quietly from tree to tree, using the trees and the darkness of the night to hide their movements. They peer around a tree and see the source of the mysterious noises. The objects on the screen are dark, yet you can see everything that's happening! How is this possible? Try this activity to learn one way it can be done.

Materials

3 pieces of blue cellophane

Procedure

1. On a sunny day, go outside. What do you see?

2. Place one piece of blue cellophane in front of your eyes. How does this change what you see?

3. Add a second piece of cellophane in front of your eyes. What effect does this have on what you see?

4. Add a third piece of cellophane in front of your eyes. What effect do the three pieces of blue cellophane have on what you see?

More Fun Stuff to Do

Try this activity, only using different colors of cellophane. How do the different colors change what you see?

Explanation

When you look outside on a sunny day, you can see all the colors of the visible spectrum—red, orange, yellow, green, blue, indigo, and violet. But when you look through the blue cellophane, most of the colors you see turn dark or even black. As you add more layers of cellophane, the scene will eventually look similar to night, but a bit brighter.

White light is actually a mixture of all the colors of the visible spectrum. When light strikes an object, some of the light is reflected and some of the light is absorbed. If an object is red, the object will reflect red light and absorb the other colors. If an object is blue, it will reflect blue and absorb the other colors. When you looked at the scene through the blue cellophane, the blue cellophane acts like a filter and will only let blue light pass through it, not the other colors. This makes all the other colors look dark. But because there is more light than at night, you will still be able to see everything.

Some movies that include a night scene will film during the day using a blue filter over the camera lens to make it seem like night. When you see these scenes in the movie, you may notice a blue tint that comes from the blue light that passes through the filter. Other movies will actually film at night but use very bright lights so that you can see the action. One problem with the second method is that to have enough artificial light to see, you end up with so much that it makes you think it's daytime.

Movie Science and Science Fiction

It's Truer Than You Think!

When you look at reruns of the original *Star Trek* television show you have to laugh at the special effects and some of the props they included in the show. Filmed in the late 1960s, the show featured such far-out futuristic ideas as a handheld communicator and a palm-size data recorder. Well, some of the science fiction of that show is the science fact of the twenty-first century, with the rapid developments in technology that have brought us cell phones and palm-size computers.

Much of what we see in movies is drawn from real science facts and from predictions that scientists make about the future. Filmmakers often turn to scientists as consultants when writing screenplays and creating costumes, props, and sets. In the movie *Mission to Mars,* for example, the movie producers used conceptual drawings made by NASA engineers that showed how astronauts might live on that planet.

Any good movie needs enough realistic facts to make it both believable and entertaining. If science is involved in the plot, then the science needs to be believable and in keeping with the science that we know.

Try the activities in this chapter to learn about the science behind many popular science fiction movies. Who knows? Maybe some of this science fiction will indeed become science fact!

PROJECT 1
Mission to Mars

In many movies about space, such as *Mission to Mars* and *2001: A Space Odyssey,* the astronauts walk around their spacecraft instead of floating as astronauts do now. How could engineers design a spacecraft that cancels out the effect of zero gravity so that people could walk around?

Materials

plastic bucket with a handle
water
an outside area

Procedure

1. Fill the bucket half full with water. What keeps the water in the bucket?

2. Slowly turn the bucket upside down over the grass. What happens to the water?

3. Fill the bucket half full with water again.

4. Hold the bucket by the handle with one hand. Start to swing the bucket, first slowly back and forth, then do full loops. What happens to the water this time?

More Fun Stuff to Do

Can you stop swinging the bucket without the water falling out? Repeat the activity. When you are doing loops, start swinging the bucket slower at the end of each swing. Return to swinging back and forth, slower and slower, until you stop the action.

Explanation

When you pour the water into the bucket, gravity, the force that pulls objects toward the earth, keeps the water at the bottom of the bucket when it is held. When the bucket is swung in a circle, the water remains in the bucket, even when the bucket is swinging upside down.

When the bucket is swinging, another force is at work, centripetal force.

Centripetal force is caused by one of Newton's Laws of Motion, the **law of inertia.** Part of this law states that moving objects keep moving in a straight line unless acted on by an outside force. Your moving arm causes the bucket and water to move. According to the law of inertia, the water in the bucket wants to move in a straight line. However, when you swing the bucket in a circle you exert an outside force on the water. For example, when you begin to swing the bucket up~~~~~ water in the bucket wants to move upward in a strai~~~~ ~~~~ bucket moves in a circle. As it moves toward ~~~~t has moved above the water and exerts a force ~~~~e water in the bucket. If you let go of the ~~~~ve the centripetal force, and the bucket, with ~~~~ a straight line.

~~~~mes into play in this activity. The force ~~~~ the bucket down, but the centripetal ~~~~motion is greater than the pull of grav-~~~~ket, even when the bucket is upside

One way to simulate gravity during a spaceflight, either real or in movies, is to have part of the spacecraft spin in a circle. This creates centripetal force. An astronaut on a spinning ship would be forced to the outside of the craft and would feel a force similar to gravity.

The movies *Mission to Mars* and *2001: A Space Odyssey* showed a spinning part of the spacecraft where astronauts could walk around. Scientists are planning a similar craft for a real mission to Mars!

PROJECT 2
Making Contact

In the movie *Contact,* Jodie Foster plays a scientist who uses radio telescopes to detect messages from outer space. We haven't gotten such a message yet, but could we?

Materials

tape recorder with microphone
yardstick (meter stick)
helper
an outside area
large mixing bowl (as large and as round as possible)

Procedure

1. Hold the microphone of the tape recorder so that it faces your helper.

2. Have your helper walk about 20 feet (6 meters) away from you and remain there throughout the experiment.

3. Ask your helper to talk in a normal tone of voice as you record what he is saying.

4. Play back the recording. How well does the recording pick up the voice?

5. Hold the bowl in front of you so that the opening of the bowl faces your helper.

6. Hold the microphone of the tape recorder so that it faces the bowl. The microphone should be at approximately the center of the bowl, at an equal distance from all sides.

7. Ask your helper to again speak in a normal tone of voice. Record what he is saying.

8. Play back the recording. How well does the recording pick up the voice this time?

More Fun Stuff to Do

Repeat the activity with the bowl, only this time hold the microphone at different distances away from the bowl. Is there a place where the recording is easiest to understand?

Explanation

The listening device you've made is called a parabolic microphone. The bowl serves as a parabolic reflector. A parabolic reflector has the ability to take sounds that strike it from a wide area and focus them at one point.

Sound waves travel through the air parallel to one another, and over distance they spread out over a large area. In the first part of this activity, when the sound waves from your helper's voice reached the microphone without the reflector, they had spread out so much through the air that only a few waves hit the microphone. When you played the recording back, your helper's voice sounded very soft. But when the sound waves from your helper hit the parabolic reflector, they bounced off the reflector at angles equal to the angles they went in. Because the parabolic reflector is curved, the reflected sound waves all meet at one point, called the focus. If the microphone is put at the focus point, it picks up the sound from all the waves that hit the bowl, not just a few. Focusing the sounds at one point makes them much louder. So when you played back the recording of your helper's voice through the parabolic microphone, his voice sounded much louder.

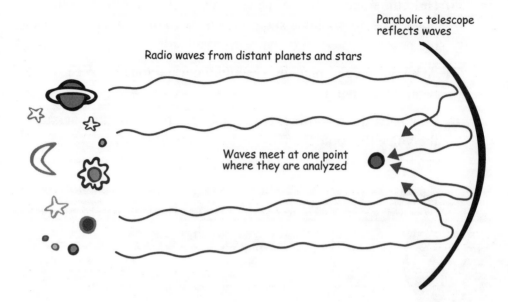

Parabolic telescope reflects waves

Radio waves from distant planets and stars

Waves meet at one point where they are analyzed

A very large version of a parabolic microphone is called a radio tele-scope. As in the movie *Contact,* astronomers have aimed groups of radio telescopes at the heavens to try and pick up messages from outer space. They have not yet been able to detect signs of intelligent life like the ones in *Contact,* but they are still listening!

PROJECT 3
Speed of Sound

In the climax of the movie *Star Wars,* Luke Skywalker successfully launches a rocket that finds its target deep inside the Death Star. Luke flies away, and in the background you see the Death Star engulfed in a ball of fire and immediately hear the explosion. Even if we assume the Death Star could exist and could have been blown up this way, why is this scene flawed? Try this activity to find out.

Materials

2 2-by-4-by-6-inch (5-by-10-by-15-cm) blocks of wood
helper
a park or other large open area

Procedure

1. Have your helper take the blocks of wood and stand about 10 feet (3 m) away from you so that she is facing you.

2. Have your helper hold one block of wood in each hand. Have her quickly and firmly bring the blocks together to make a loud noise. Note when you saw the blocks come together and when you heard the sound they made.

3. Next, have your helper move at least 150 yards (135 m) away to a place where you can still see her clearly. Again have your helper strike the blocks together. Note when you saw the blocks come together and when you heard the sound they made.

Explanation

When the helper was 10 feet (3 m) away, you heard the sound the blocks made at the same time that you saw them hit each other. However, when your helper was 150 yards (135 m) away, you saw the blocks strike each other a fraction of a second before you heard the sound.

Light travels at a very fast speed, 186,000 miles per second (300,000 kilometers per second). It takes almost no time for you to see the two blocks strike each other. Sound, on the other hand, travels much more slowly in air, 1,090 feet (330 meters) per second. The sound made by the blocks striking each other takes a fraction of a second longer to reach you than the light reflected off the blocks as they hit each other. The farther you are from the striking blocks, the longer the time between when you see the blocks strike each other and the time when you hear them.

In the *Star Wars* movie mentioned in the opening to this activity, Luke Skywalker would have had to get at least 10,000 kilometers away from the Death Star when it exploded to avoid being blown up with it. He would have almost instantly seen the Death Star explode, but it would have taken over eight hours for him to hear the explosion! And that's only if sound could travel in space, which it can't! Sound needs air molecules to travel, and in space there are no molecules, so sound would not travel at all.

PROJECT 4
Worm Holes

The captain gives the order to go to warp speed and enter the worm hole. The plan is to use the worm hole to reach the far side of the galaxy in time to save the dying planet. Could this ever happen? And what is a worm hole? Try this activity to learn more about them.

Materials

paper   ruler

pencil   penny

Procedure

1. Place the paper horizontally on a table and use the ruler to draw a straight line 6 inches (15 cm) long near the center of the paper.

2. Place the penny on the line near one end of the paper. Move the penny along the line to the other end. This represents the trip of a spaceship from one end of a galaxy to the other.

3. Hold one end of the paper in each hand.

4. Move your hands together so that a wrinkle forms in the paper below your hands. Continue to move the paper until the two ends of the line are close together. Now imagine the penny traveling from one end of the line to the other.

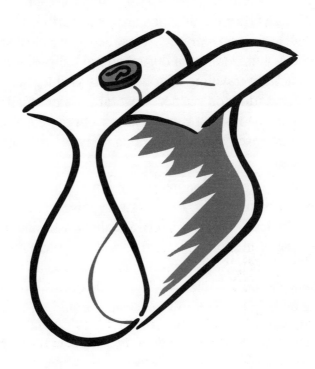

Explanation

Creating a wrinkle in the paper brought the two ends of the line closer together. So instead of traveling along the whole line to get from one end to the other, the penny could travel over the wrinkle and get from one end to the other faster.

In this example, you saw two different physicists' views of space and time. Sir Isaac Newton saw space as being like the first model, like a flat piece of paper, while Albert Einstein saw space as being like the second model, with wrinkles and curves in it. Newton saw a universe where objects traveled in straight lines unless acted on by an outside force. His flat model of space could be used to explain much of what scientists saw in the universe.

But Einstein saw a different universe, where space was curved by the gravity of large objects, such as planets and stars. Einstein believed that this curved space would influence everything, from the motion of comets to the path light takes from distant stars. When Einstein first put forth this theory, most scientists didn't fully believe him. In 1919, to support his theory, Einstein predicted that the path light would travel from a distant star would curve as it passed near the sun, due to the sun's gravity. This theory, was tested by British astronomer Arthur Eddington during a total eclipse of the sun, a time when the starlight traveling near the sun is visible. Scientists waited anxiously for Eddington's report, several staying up all night in anticipation of the results. But Einstein went to bed. When the results were released the next morning, they were exactly as Einstein had predicted.

Since that time some astronomers, but not all, have theorized that if space were curved enough, by say a very large heavenly body, then it could fold back on itself. This could allow astronauts to travel from one side of the fold to the other without having to travel the distance in between. Such a curve has become known as a worm hole. Science fiction movies rely on the theory of worm holes a lot because they help explain how spaceships could quickly cover very long distances.

PROJECT 5
Tidal Forces

In the movie *Independence Day,* an alien mother ship that is about one-fourth the size of the moon stations itself above Earth's surface. It readies itself to attack Earth by launching small saucers. But would that really be necessary? What effects would an orbiting spaceship that size have on Earth? Try the next activity to find out.

Materials

18-inch (45-cm) piece of thin, stiff wire (the wire should be thin enough to easily bend into a circle, but stiff enough to return to its circular shape when pulled lightly and released)

tape	pencil
white paper	8-inch (20-cm) piece of string
12-inch (30-cm)	ruler
square piece of cardboard	scissors
colored pencils or markers	marble
pushpins	

Procedure

1. Bend the wire into a circle. Connect the ends of the wire by overlapping them about ½ inch (1.25 cm) and taping them in place.

2. Tape a piece of white paper to the middle of the cardboard.

3. Draw a circle, about 4 inches (10 cm) in diameter, in the center of the paper. Color the circle so it looks like Earth.

4. Place the wire circle around the circle you have drawn. Push the pushpin into the cardboard so it touches the inside of the top of the wire circle.

5. Tie the center of the string around the wire circle at a point directly across from the pushpin.

6. Measure and cut both ends of the string so that each end of string extends 3 inches (7.5 cm) from the wire.

7. Tape one end of the string to the center of the circle you have drawn on the paper. This string should be loose. Tape the other end to a marble.

8. Pull the marble away from the paper circle until the string attached to the middle of the paper circle is straight. What happens to the shape of the wire around the paper circle?

Explanation

The circle of wire should change shape and become an oval. The oval will be farther away from the top and bottom of the circle on the paper and closer to the sides.

The water on the surface of Earth moves in a way similar to the way the wire moves. This creates the tides. **Tides** are changes in the distribution of water on Earth caused by the gravity of the moon and sun pulling on Earth. The marble represents the moon and the push-pin represents the sun.

But what does this have to do with *Independence Day* and the attack of the mother ship? Well, if the mother ship had actually been as large as they said it was and was very close to Earth, it too would have had a gravitational effect on the ocean and tides. The tides

would have been much, much higher than normal, probably flooding all the coastal areas it flew above. New York and Washington would have been destroyed by water, so the smaller saucers would not have been necessary!

PROJECT 6
Attack of the 15-Foot Baby

In the movie *Honey, I Blew Up the Kid*, the hero creates a device that makes his baby's body suddenly grow to 15 feet (4 m). But what other changes would this increase in height bring? Try this activity to find out.

Materials

cardboard toilet paper roll   several books
cardboard paper towel roll

Procedure

1. Place the toilet paper roll on end on the table.

2. Carefully balance one book on top of it. Keep adding books one at a time until the roll collapses. How many books can it hold?

3. Next, place the paper towel roll on end on the table.

4. Carefully balance one book on the top of it. Keep adding books one at a time until the roll collapses. How many books can it hold? Which roll can hold more weight?

More Fun Stuff to Do

Place two paper towel rolls on end next to each other. Balance one book on top of both. Keep adding books, one at a time, until the paper towel rolls collapse. Does twice the amount of support material hold more weight?

Explanation

The toilet paper roll, which is shorter, should hold more weight than the longer paper towel roll. And two paper towel rolls will hold more weight than one.

The ability of a long object such as a paper towel or a toilet paper roll, or the bones in the human thigh, to support weight on their ends depends in part on their cross-sectional area. Cross-sectional area is the amount of area you would have if you cut through it at a right angle. If something doubles in size, it does so in all directions—length, width, and height. This causes an increase in mass that is eight times the original mass ($2 \times 2 \times 2 = 8$; twice the size in each direction). But the cross-sectional area, which is where the strength of the legs comes from, increases only four times.

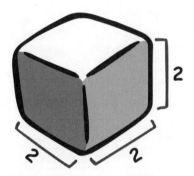

VOLUME = 2x2x2=8
CROSS SECTIONAL AREA=
2x2=4

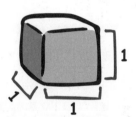

VOLUME = 1x1x1=1
CROSS SECTIONAL AREA=
1x1=1

If a normal baby is 3 feet tall, a 15-foot baby would be 5 times taller than normal and would also be 5 times wider and 5 times bigger from front to back. This would give it 125 times the original mass ($5 \times 5 \times 5 = 125$; 5 times in each direction), but the legs would only be 25 times as strong and would probably break under the extra weight.

A similar problem would occur with the giant mutant insects so popular in 1950s movies. The enlarged insect would not be able to stand up on its legs!

PROJECT

Building Dinos

In the movie *Jurassic Park,* scientists use the DNA they find in blood from ancient mosquitoes to create dinosaurs. If scientists could really get dinosaur blood using this technique, could they actually use it to create a living dinosaur? Try this activity to find out.

Materials

paper
pencil

Procedure

1. Write out the coded message below on the paper.

A G T A C G G G G T C G G A C G A T A C T C A G A C G

2. Draw a vertical line after every third letter. This should divide the letters into nine groups of three letters.

3. Translate each three-letter sequence, using the code below:

ACT—A	ACG—R	CCC—P	TCG—W	CAG—I
AGT—B	ATC—T	AAA—S	TTC—X	GAC—N
AAA—C	TCA—D	GGG—O	CAT—E	GAT—H

What does the message say?

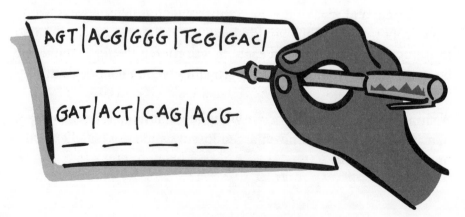

More Fun Stuff to Do
Use the three-letter sequences to write other words.

Explanation

The translation of the coded message should be BROWN HAIR.

This activity is similar to how messages are contained in DNA. Each of your body's cells contains 46 chromosomes made of DNA, deoxyribonucleic acid. Your DNA contains a code of over 3 billion "letters" with information that determines your hair color, skin color, height, and over 100,000 different things. The variations in this code make each of us unique.

DNA uses a sequence of chemicals called nucleic acids to make genes. A **gene** is a part of a chromosome that produces a specific trait in an individual. The order of these chemicals, like the order of the letters in a code, determines your traits. There are only four **nucleic acids**—adenine (A), guanine (G), thymine (T), and cytosine (C). Each chromosome contains a long sequence of these four letters. Three letters in a row form a **codon,** a code for a different chemical. In our simulation, they represented a letter. The chemicals from these codons link together to form one gene or trait, such as having brown hair.

Scientists have been working on one of history's great scientific milestones—to decode the 3 billion chemical "letters" in human DNA. Called the Human Genome Project, it has taken thousands of scientists working with powerful computers and sophisticated robotic instruments to determine the code of human DNA. But that is only the first step. It could take another century to break the code into genes and then figure out exactly what each gene does!

So, could scientists do the same thing for dinosaurs? Sure, but they would have to determine a code for that creature as well. The real problem is that the long strands of DNA begin to break into smaller fragments after about 30 years. The chances that DNA that is 65 million years old will still be intact are remote—even if we could find it!

PROJECT 8
The Man with X-Ray Eyes

Superman and some other superheroes are supposed to have "X-ray vision." X-ray vision allows the superhero to look through walls or to see weapons concealed in a pocket. But is X-ray vision possible? Try this next activity to find out.

Materials

flashlight
dark room

Procedure

1. Hold the fingers of one hand together and look at the back of your hand. Notice what you see.

2. Turn on the flashlight and turn off all the lights in the room.

3. Holding your fingers together, place your fingers palm down over the light of the flashlight. What do you see this time?

Explanation

Even though your "X ray" is ordinary light and not real X rays, the effect is similar. Your hand will appear red, and you may be able to see dark rods in the middle of your fingers.

Light is made up of more than just the visible light that we see. Visible light is part of the electromagnetic spectrum, which also includes infrared light, ultraviolet light, microwaves, television and radio waves, and even X rays. When light hits your fingers, it passes

through skin and muscle and it appears red. But some of the light also hits the bones in your fingers. The light rays cannot pass through your bones, so the bones in your fingers look like dark rods. When you have an X ray taken at the doctor's office, the X-ray light works in a similar way. When the X rays hit skin and muscle, they pass right through it and appear dark when they strike photographic film. But the X rays cannot pass through bone. Bones appear white on the photographic film.

One problem with X-ray vision is that our eyes are not capable of sending out any light, including X rays. Our eyes are receivers of light, not senders. But even if they were senders of light, our eyes would have to both send and receive the X rays, and be on opposite sides of the object at the same time!

Glossary

acid—a substance that reacts with a base to form a salt

amplify—make louder

auditory canal—tube that connects and directs the sound vibrations from the pinna to the delicate parts of the ear located inside your head

auditory nerve—the nerve that transmits nerve impulses from the ear to the brain, where the sound is identified

base—a substance that reacts with an acid to form a salt

biology—the field of science that studies the origin, history, and characteristics of plants and animals

chemical indicator—a special substance that, when mixed with an acid or a base, will change color

chemical reaction—a change in matter in which substances break apart to form new substances

chemistry—the science that investigates matter

cochlea—a fluid-filled chamber in the inner ear that contains specialized hair cells that respond to sound waves of different vibrations

codon—three nucleic acids in a row that represent one "letter" in a code and link to form one gene or trait

crystals—the regular shape that some solids have

density—the ratio of the mass of an object to its volume

DNA—deoxyribonucleic acid

ear canal—another name for the auditory canal

eardrum—part of the ear that moves when sound vibrations hit it

electrons—parts of the atom that revolve around the nucleus of the atom and have a negative charge

foley artist—the person who adds sound effects to films, television, radio shows, and live plays to make their stories realistic

force—a push or pull

forced perspective—a kind of optical illusion that occurs because your brain incorrectly interprets something you are seeing as being similar to what you've seen before

fulcrum—the fixed point that a lever rotates around

gene—part of a chromosome that produces a specific trait

gravity—the force of attraction between all objects

hypothesis—an educated guess about the results of an experiment you are going to perform

index of refraction—the amount that light refracts, or bends, when traveling from one transparent substance to another

inner ear—part of the ear that contains the cochlea and auditory nerve

kinetic energy—energy that is being used

law of inertia—a law stating that moving objects keep moving in a straight line unless acted on by an outside force

lever—a simple machine made up of a rigid board or bar that is supported at a fixed point

middle ear—the eardrum plus three small bones that move to amplify sound. These bones are called the **hammer,** the **anvil,** and the **stirrup,** so named because of their shapes.

nucleic acids—four chemicals, adenine (A), guanine (G), thymine (T), and cytosine (C), whose order determines unique genetic characteristics

optics—the study of how light behaves

outer ear—part of the ear composed of the outer ear flap

parabolic reflector—a reflector that has the ability to focus sounds at one point

Pascal's principle—a principle of fluids stating that if pressure is exerted on one part of a fluid, then the pressure is transmitted equally everywhere in the fluid

persistence of vision—a process where an image is retained on the retina of your eye for a fraction of a second

pheromone—a chemical that animals can smell and are attracted to

photography—the way some pictures are made, using the chemical action of light on special surfaces such as film

physics—the science of matter and energy and how they interact

physiology—the branch of biology that studies the function of organisms, like humans, and their organs

pinna—the outer flap of the ear; what you commonly call the ear

plasma—the liquid part of blood that is mainly salt water

platelets—special blood cells that help blood clot to heal cuts and tears

potential energy—energy that is stored for later use

prism—a transparent object that bends light

protons—parts of the atom found in the nucleus of an atom and having a positive charge

red blood cells—special blood cells that carry oxygen to all of the cells in the body and carry carbon dioxide away

reflection—the bouncing of light as it strikes the surface of different materials

refracts—the bending of light as it moves from one transparent substance to another

scientific method—a way to perform an experiment involving a hypothesis, an experiment, analyzing the results, and drawing a conclusion

simple machine—a device that helps you to do work more easily

sound—energy that we can hear

spectrum—the colors that make up white light: red, orange, yellow, green, blue, indigo, and violet

static electricity—electricity that does not flow

sublimation—when a solid turns directly into a gas without turning into a liquid first

tides—changes in the distribution of water on Earth caused by the gravity of the moon and sun pulling on Earth

vision—the way your eyes and brain work together that makes you think you see certain images

vibration—moving rapidly up and down

white blood cells—special blood cells that help the body fight infection and disease

Index